The Millionaire Fast

Uncovering The Wells

Coral Aguilar

SDO Group Publishers

THE MILLIONAIRE FAST

Uncovering The Wells

Copyright © 2025 by Coral Aguilar

Brownsville, Texas

info@coralaguilar.com

All rights reserved

ISBN: 979-8-9993227-0-8

Published by

SDO Group Publishers

Brownsville, Texas

Acknowledgments

T his book was birthed through a journey of revelation, persistence, and radical faith. I want to take a moment to express my deepest gratitude to the people who helped make it possible.

To my heavenly Father — every insight, every page, and every well uncovered is for Your glory. Thank You for allowing me to steward this message.

To my husband, Pablo, your unwavering belief in me and in the call on my life gives me the confidence to run boldly. Thank you for leading our family with vision and faith. You are my biggest encourager, best strategist, and closest friend.

To my children — your laughter and love are my daily motivation. May you always pursue the wells God has placed within you.

To the spiritual sons and daughters of our house — thank you for walking this faith journey with me. Your hunger for growth continues to inspire me to write, teach, and pour out.

To every early reader, editor, and friend who believed in this project — your prayers, critiques, and encouragement have helped sharpen the message and elevate its reach.

To my dad, Victor Garcia, and my uncle, Meliton Garcia, for believing in this project and investing in it financially to make it a reality.

And finally, to the reader — thank you for opening this book. I pray you not only read it, but that you run with it. There is a well waiting to be uncovered on your journey to the fast lane.

With love and gratitude — Coral Aguilar

Foreword

by Pastor Jaime Loya

I've known Coral for many years as a woman of deep faith, profound passion, and uncommon perseverance. When she first shared her vision for this project with me, I knew immediately that it was going to be a game changer. This isn't just another book about fasting & faith — Coral Aguilar has given us a blueprint that shows us how to unlock the hidden potential God has placed on the inside of each and every one of us.

The title itself, *The Millionaire Fast*, catches your attention. At first, it sounds like a book about wealth or success. But as you read, you will discover that this book isn't about chasing money — it's about uncovering the spiritual wealth already placed inside of you. It's about discovering that fasting isn't simply depriving yourself of food but aligning yourself with God's perfect will for your life!

One of the things I admire most about Coral is her dedication. She doesn't just teach fasting — she lives it. Year after year, she's modeled the discipline of fasting and prayer in her ministry, her marriage, and her family. I've seen firsthand the fruit of that faithfulness. Every chapter of this book bears witness to it — the miracles, the answered prayers, the dreams that were birthed because she dared to believe that God could do more.

From the very first page, Coral invites you on a journey that is both personal and prophetic. She doesn't write from theory; she writes from her very own testimony. Each chapter flows from real experiences of waiting, wrestling, believing, and ultimately witnessing God's mighty hand. That's the "millionaire" status she's inviting you into; a life that is filled with God's goodness and glory. It's about overflowing with vision, being rich in character, and prospering in every area.

As a pastor, I've seen many people pray for change without preparing for it. We want God to bless us but are not willing to pay the price that comes with it. That's why I love this book! Coral doesn't sugarcoat the process. She tells you the hard truth: that fasting will test you, stretch you, and confront you, but she also shows you that on the other side of that discomfort is breakthrough, blessings, favor and supernatural acceleration.

One of the most profound aspects of Coral's message is her understanding that fasting removes the weights that slow us down from fulfilling our God-given purpose. Her insight is biblical, yet practical. Her tone is pastoral, yet powerful. She doesn't simply tell you to fast, she teaches you how to fast with purpose, how to tag your fast with faith, and how to win your battles using fasting as a spiritual weapon.

She writes about fasting as a tool for transformation, she calls it "the process of extraction in the spirit" — removing what's unnecessary so only what's essential can rise to the surface. Because before God can trust you with more, He often must strip away what no longer serves your purpose. Coral shows you how fasting becomes that refining fire, preparing you to handle the blessings you've been praying for.

What makes this book especially powerful is the way it speaks to *every kind of reader*. Whether you're a leader like me trying to accomplish your vision, a new believer seeking to deepen your intimacy with God, or simply someone ready for a personal reset—this book gives you the tools and the truth to start seeing change today.

Coral reminds us that the true "fast lane" is not about doing more—it's about becoming more, becoming whole, becoming strong, and becoming who God originally designed us to be. It isn't just about going faster; it's about going deeper. Because when you discover the true wealth within, you'll step into the kind of life God always intended for you: fruitful, purposeful, and overflowing with His goodness.

As you turn these pages, I encourage you to do more than read—respond. Let the Holy Spirit speak to you through Coral's words. Let them challenge the areas of your life that have grown dull and complacent. Let them call you back to the secret place where the true riches of heaven are found. Don't just read this book, experience it. Fast with it. Pray through it. Let it take you deeper than you've ever gone before.

If you are tired of living beneath your potential... if you sense that there's more inside of you like a hidden treasure waiting to be unearthed, then this book is for you. If you've ever felt stuck, empty, or unsure of what's next, this book is your invitation to start fresh. Coral is proof that when you commit your body, mind, and spirit to God through fasting, He will take you places you never imagined.

My prayer is that as you read this book, your hunger for God will increase. That you'll start to see fasting as a blessing not as a burden. That you'll begin to unlock the wells of hope, joy, love, peace and purpose that have been waiting to flow again.

So, get ready! Because as you fast, as you pray, and as you pursue God with all your heart, you're not just going to go farther; you're going to live fuller. You will soon uncover the wells of wealth and realize that you've been rich all along. You're going to find the treasure that's been buried in you since the beginning of time. May *The Millionaire Fast* challenge you, stretch you, and ultimately change you.

— Pastor Jaime Loya

Founder & Senior Pastor, Cross Church – San Benito, Texas

Founder & President of 360° Global Network

Preface

C atchy title, huh? "The Millionaire Fast".

The millionaire fast is a concept that true wealth extends beyond material possessions. The book is not about financial riches but the priceless assets in one's life—family, time, faith, and personal growth. Fasting like a millionaire is a mindset that you must adopt because successful people have a different way of seeing things and doing things. Just as a financial millionaire doesn't settle for the ordinary discipline in their business, you must refuse mediocrity in any area of your life.

You normally wouldn't associate fasting, a health-spiritual concept, with money or riches. So, let's address the elephant in the room before anything else; this book is not intended to instruct you on how to fast to reach a net worth of $1,000,000. I cannot tell you that I fasted, and camels loaded with gold coins suddenly appeared. So why then the title?

Fasting is not just a spiritual discipline; it is a powerful tool for achieving clarity, focus, and personal transformation. For centuries, high achievers in various fields—whether entrepreneurs, athletes, or leaders—have understood that true success begins with self-discipline. By mastering the art of fasting, they tap into a mindset that prioritizes mental clarity, emotional resilience, and the ability to rise above distractions. This practice isn't simply about abstaining from food; it's about cultivating the inner strength needed to persevere and succeed, even when faced with adversity. Fasting allows us to align with higher goals, refine our purpose, and gain the energy needed to achieve extraordinary things.

Fasting is the key that unlocks the true person and potential that you have inside. You have not met the best version of yourself yet, so this book will challenge you to do things differently, and you most definitely will have different results.

Contents

Key Terms & Biblical Fasts

Fast: To abstain from food or drink for a determined amount of time.

Spiritual Fasting: Is a spiritual discipline that trains your mind and body to tune out distractions and focus on hearing God more clearly.

Types of Fasts in the Bible & Their Outcomes

Fasting is a recurring theme throughout the Bible, often linked to spiritual breakthroughs, divine guidance, and supernatural intervention. Here are some of the most significant fasts in Scripture, along with their outcomes:

1. The 40-Day Fast of Jesus

- Reference: Matthew 4:1-11, Luke 4:1-13

- Type: Absolute Fast (No food, only water)

- Outcome: Jesus overcame Satan's temptations and began His public ministry in power and authority.

2. The Daniel Fast

- Reference: Daniel 1:8-16, Daniel 10:2-3

- Type: Partial Fast (No meat, wine, or rich foods; only vegetables and water)

- Outcome: Increased wisdom, revelation, and favor. In Daniel 10, after a 21-day fast, an angel brought him divine understanding.

3. The Esther Fast (3-Day Fast)

- Reference: Esther 4:15-17

- Type: Absolute Fast (No food or water for 3 days)

- Outcome: Divine favor led to the deliverance of the Jewish people from destruction.

4. The Nineveh Fast (Corporate 3-Day Fast / Repentance)

- Reference: Jonah 3:5-10

- Type: Absolute Fast (The entire city, including animals,

abstained from food and water)

- Outcome: God spared Nineveh from destruction due to their repentance.

A Word of Wisdom Before You Fast

While fasting is a powerful spiritual discipline that anyone can practice, it's important to seek guidance. I encourage you to ask the Holy Spirit for direction on the type of fast that aligns with your journey. Additionally, if you have any medical conditions or are taking medication, consult your doctor before beginning an extended fast. Fasting should be done with wisdom, faith, and preparation.

Introduction

J ust last night, I found myself laughing at the thought, "I can't believe I have another baby!" You must hear the tone, though—I laughed in awe, because what once seemed impossible has now become possible. Here's what I mean. I need you to feel what I'm feeling. I'm truly amazed! To understand the depth of this emotion, let me take you on a journey into my world, a world where the concept of the The Millionaire Fast unfolded, not in financial gains, but in the richness of life's most precious assets.

I got married very young. I was only seventeen when I got engaged, turned eighteen in September, and was married by October. My husband and I only dated for two months then he gave me my princess wedding. I know it all sounds rushed as I tell it, but honestly, in real life, it felt perfect.

I want to make something clear: I didn't get married because I was pregnant. I didn't have my firstborn until I was 21. And I must admit, I still feel favored just to say "firstborn." It reminds me of the angel's salutation to Mary: "Greetings, favored woman! The Lord is with you!" (Luke 1:28 NLT).

After my daughter turned five, we were ready to try for another baby. We tried month after month, year after year, but it was always negative. According to my gynecologist, everything was functioning properly. After countless attempts, I began to accept that my destiny might be a small family. I came to terms with the fact that I was meant to have just one child. It was tough, especially since I come from a family of five. My siblings all have more than one child—my oldest sibling has five, my sister has four, the next brother has five as well, and the youngest of the boys has two. I was the only one with just one child. My husband comes from a large family too, with six siblings in total.

In the first few years of trying to conceive our second child, I bought pregnancy test after pregnancy test, but after a while, it started to feel hopeless. I eventually stopped checking. By then, my daughter was fourteen, and even if we conceived another child, I thought the age gap was already too great. We decided to stop trying. I thought to myself, if it happens, it happens. If it doesn't, well, that's okay. I am already blessed.

After a fourteen-year journey marked by setbacks, mental decluttering, and transformative shifts, we finally conceived our second child. I am certain that we've connected with something extraordinary—almost supernatural—a phenomenon that can only be described as a miracle, accomplished through the Master Creator-God, by fasting!

1

Rediscover Your Potential

"But when you fast, anoint your head and wash
your face, so that your fasting may not be seen by
others but by your Father who is in secret. And
your Father who sees in secret will reward you."
Matthew 6:17-18 (ESV)

The Beginning of a Journey

E very year, I start with a 21-day Daniel's Fast—a practice I've
maintained since 2009. This journey began when my pastor,
Apostle Juan De La Garza, introduced me to the fast. It made such
an impact that it became a core principle in my lifestyle.

Let me give you some context: I'm the type of person who
constantly challenges herself. I live by the motto, *"In order to have*

what you've never had, you must do what you've never done". After doing *The Daniel's Fast* for ten consecutive years, I reached a point where it no longer felt challenging. I realized that for something to be a true sacrifice, it must stretch and hurt—and my fast wasn't doing that anymore.

Around that time, I began reading *Supernatural Business* by Mike Rovner. From the foreword, I was captivated. Rovner's description of living with total surrender resonated deeply with me. He spoke about giving until it hurts—a concept I hadn't fully embraced but instantly understood. Inspired by his faith, I decided to adopt this principle in my life. I wanted to become a person known for waking up every day and saying "*Yes!*" to purpose.

This reflection reminded me of King David's offering in 2 Samuel 24:24. When David was offered a gift for his sacrifice, he insisted on paying for it, saying, "*I will not present burnt offerings to the LORD my God that have cost me nothing.*" True sacrifice comes with a price, and I was ready to pay it.

The Challenge of Fasting

When I first attempted *The Daniel's Fast*, it was a genuine struggle. As a Mexican, my diet revolved around flavorful dishes like *taquitos, enchiladas,* and *caldo de pollo*—foods that are far from vegan. Those of you that know me personally will not let me lie—I love to eat! I eat more than my husband, which is saying something considering he's 6 feet tall and a solid 210 pounds. Meanwhile, I'm over here at 5'3 and 120 pounds, defying all logic. God does work in mysterious ways. Laugh it's good for you.

All kidding aside, adjusting to a plant-based diet was painful, especially for someone like me who enjoys savoring every bite of food, particularly the ones containing meats and cheese. But through the discomfort, I discovered the discipline necessary to control my cravings.

Fast forward to 2020, I felt God calling me to go deeper. That year, I completed my first 21-day juice fast, consuming only water and freshly squeezed juices. This fast pushed me beyond my limits. By the end, I felt a renewed sense of purpose and energy. It reminded me that true growth often comes from stepping into the unknown and embracing discomfort. The day I finished, I remember asking my husband, 'You didn't think I could do it, did you?' He replied, 'I didn't think—I knew you would."

Why Juicing?

I knew that I needed something different because I ended the previous year feeling completely drained—low on both energy and creativity. I had intended to finish strong, but the truth is, I was utterly exhausted.

Juicing still aligns with the principles of *The Daniel's Fast* but adds a new layer of discipline. Unlike blending, juicing extracts the liquid while discarding the solid fibers, making it more challenging. The hunger intensifies, and the fast becomes an even greater sacrifice. However, the benefits—both physical and spiritual—make it worthwhile.

Breaking the Stronghold of Food

It's crazy how food changes you. It has so much influence on your identity. A person that has a well-balanced diet for the most part will feel comfortable with their weight, which directly influences their self-esteem. If you feel good about yourself, you gain confidence, and your personality will be that of a positive optimistic individual. On the other hand, a person who consistently lacks a balanced diet may struggle with their weight, leading to dissatisfaction and a negative impact on self-esteem. When you don't feel good about yourself, your confidence drops, often resulting in a more pessimistic and withdrawn outlook on life.

Many of us form a stronghold or dependency on food—especially food that isn't good for us—as a source of comfort, only to realize later that it's become a barrier to our health, energy, and overall well-being.

At the start of the year, many of us seek a reset. We want to shed the heaviness of the past and embrace a fresh start. Juicing provides a physical detox, removing toxins that drain energy and creativity. With each day of the fast, you notice increased energy, mental clarity, and motivation. The transformation is undeniable—and it's just the beginning.

The Power of Fasting

While the physical benefits of fasting are impressive, the spiritual rewards are unparalleled. Today, spirituality is trending, and many seek to connect with a higher power. But true connection comes through the Creator, not creation.

Not all avenues take you to meet your creator. You may have contact with creation, but there is nothing like meeting your creator face to face. Answer this question; who do you think knows you best, your creator, the architect that made every part of you with a specific function or the creation that is learning its capabilities as it goes? If you really want to know how a product works and its purpose the best person to ask is the inventor.

What I'm trying to say is that it is not enough to want to get more spiritual, you must take the correct route. The Bible teaches that the only way to the Father is through Jesus. By fasting, we position ourselves to hear His voice, align with His will, and step into our God-given purpose.

If you picked up this book, it's because you're ready for a change. You're ready to embrace habits that will extract the essence of the Spirit within you. This book isn't here to attack your beliefs but to challenge you to grow. Growth requires bravery and a willingness to step into the unknown.

Not all avenues take you to meet your creator.

The Seed Within You

- Do you believe you have already met the best version of yourself?

- Do you believe you have already seen all that you were created to be?

Have you ever considered the potential of a single seed?

An orange seed has the potential to produce 300 oranges per season. There are orange trees that continue to produce fruit even after 100 years. So, an orange seed can produce up to 30,000 oranges in its lifetime.

I'm talking about one seed that weighs 145 milligrams and is one centimeter in size. If this small matter has the power to produce so many riches, where does that leave you? Think about it. The Bible says you were created to be fruitful and multiply. God gave humanity an order to fill the earth. He didn't say fill the region or this small area. He said fill the earth. Make it rich. Come on! If that doesn't give you a clearer picture of the power hidden within you then I don't know what will?

All this power is contained within the seed, yet its potential remains dormant until it is planted in the right environment. Similarly, you carry untapped potential that will only materialize when you step out of your comfort zone and embrace the process of growth.

Remember that a seed in a drawer has the same potential as a seed in the soil. I ask you—have you been hiding in the drawer, keeping yourself in the safe zone or have you taken the risk of being planted? Yes, there is a risk because just like the seed, there are areas of yourself that you will have to die to in order to see the manifestation of that hidden power.

Being planted isn't easy. Just like a seed must die to its old form to sprout and reach the light, we must let go of our old selves to step into our God-ordained destiny. This process requires faith, courage, and a willingness to endure discomfort.

Putting the Seed to Work

Let's explore the incredible potential of a single orange seed:

- This seed can grow into a tree that produces oranges, which can be sold for profit.

- The harvested oranges can be transformed into orange juice, distributed in grocery stores.

- The seed can also be the start of a farm, creating a grove of orange trees that provide jobs for many people.

- Alternatively, it can inspire a small business, such as a juice bar, bringing blessings and opportunities to a handful of people.

- Oranges from the seed can be used as ingredients in famous cake recipes or crafted into popular candies sold worldwide.

Let's unpack this further—If a seed can move a mountain what makes you think that you cannot? The seed literally dies to what it knows, and it resurrects into what it was meant to become. It pushes the soil out of the way so it can see the light. In this case there is no light at the end of the tunnel. There is nothing but darkness. It seeks what it can't see and makes it to the light one push at a time. This reminds me of the chapter *'Seeking What You Can't See'* in my previous book, *Self-Doubt Out: God's Masterpiece.*

The seed grows up because it was predestined to grow up. It was engineered this way.

Just like that seed, there is predetermined greatness that makes you the richest person on this earth. It will take a courageous individual that is willing to die to their old self and be born again to become Christ-like. You embrace self-denial. You pick up your cross and follow Him.

Breaking Free from the Comfort Zone

If you are looking for comfort, this book isn't for you!

Comfort may feel safe, but it's a prison that stifles growth. It doesn't let you evolve into the next phase of your purpose. It is erroneous to think that doing the same thing over and over will give you different results. There is no way!

To experience transformation, you must break free from routines that no longer serve you. As Craig Groeschel writes in *The Power to Change*, success isn't about trying harder but about training consistently. A shift in mindset leads to lasting change.

Some people's diet consists of fast food, while others diet consists of organic homemade meals. One way you can determine a person's lifestyle is by looking at their diet. That will tell a big portion of their story. Again, by diet I don't mean a temporary change that will give you temporary results. I mean something that forms part of you which has molded you to be who you are now. When it comes to habits, to be successful, you must stop trying and start training. The result of trying is failure every time no matter how hard you try, but when you train you win every day.

For instance, if you're trying to lose weight, it's not enough to simply want it. You need to make tangible changes in your diet and exercise routine. Remember, it doesn't start with the action itself; it starts with your mind. You will have to redefine life and what you want to get out of it. If you don't have a mind shift you will not see change. Then, once you've had this mind shift, you will have to apply the action necessary.

If you're satisfied with where you are, this might seem like a good time to stop reading. Don't get me wrong—it's fine to feel happy about your achievements. But you can't stay there. Why not? Isn't it a good place? Here's the key: accomplishments, while valuable and worth celebrating, are like important historical events—they belong to the past. Purpose, however, always lies ahead of you.

My husband taught me a great truth, he said,

"Accomplishment can be the graveyard of your next dream, or it can be the monument to your potential."

Accomplishment cannot be your place of habitation. You must continue striving for the next milestone in your life's journey. You have an entire life ahead to become the God-given image uniquely designed for you. You might say, "I'm too old, and I don't have much time." If that's the case, then there's even greater urgency to live the life you were sent to this earth to fulfill.

Fasting Brings Out Your Character

I'm happy to see how far God has allowed me to go. The processes I've lived through have molded me into a woman of character—one who will not be influenced by the storms of life. A person of character is someone with a solid foundation, not like the waves tossed *to and fro*. A person of character does not let their emotions lead but is purpose driven.

Let me give you a quick example. In the study guide *Do the New You* by Steven Furtick, he asks the question: "*Can you think of any times in the past when you had to choose to do what was right, even though your circumstances or emotions made it difficult?*" This was my response:

"I'm currently there. My mind says, '*Quit.*' My heart says, '*Move away.*' But my faith says, '*Follow me.*'"

When you go through storms or dark valleys, it's easy to be led by what you see and feel. Your greatest desire in those moments is to take the easy way out. But when it comes to character, you don't do what's easy—you do what's right. When it comes to character, you don't think about yourself; you think about the greater good for everyone.

**But when it comes to character, you don't do
what's easy—you do what's right.**

I want to help you build a Christ-like character. One that isn't identified by a job, or a title but by the greater purpose. You see I am a mom, but that is not my purpose. I am a pastor but that is not my purpose. I am a business owner but that is not my purpose. My husband is a director in our local university but that is not his purpose. All of this is part of the assignment. The greater purpose is to glorify our Creator through our different assignments. There is a verse in the Bible that says, *"Let your light so shine before men, that they may see your good works, and glorify your Father which is in heaven."* (Mathew 5:16 KJV)

The different roles we play are meant to impact a specific people-group or area. The panoramic picture points everything to Jesus which is the door that leads us to the Creator of the universe. I have heard so many people call the universe God. The truth is that the universe is a part of creation, it is not the creator. You may ask, so then what should I call God? Well, the Bible tells us that God chose a certain family to identify themselves as God's children. It was the family of Israel that he trusted with His name and His laws. It is through the children of Israel that we get the name Yahweh or Jehovah which means *"I Am"*. I believe what God was trying to say was *"don't limit me to a name"*. We learn this from the Hebrew Bible.

You may ask how do we know that the Bible is the truth? How reliable is this source? Faith will be necessary when you read this book. Not one of us was there when the book was written, but we have the faith to believe that the authors were inspired by God to give us this message. Faith is simply not being able to see with your eyes but believing with your heart.

Many of the authors of the Bible did not write from their own wisdom, but through divine inspiration—often during seasons of fasting, prayer, and seeking God's presence. Moses, who wrote the foundational books of the Bible, fasted for 40 days on Mount Sinai before receiving the commandments that would shape God's covenant with His people (Exodus 34:28). Daniel, known for his wisdom and prophetic revelations, fasted regularly, including a 21-day fast that led to a divine visitation and insight into future events (Daniel 10:2-3).

Prophets like Jeremiah and Ezra called for fasting during times of repentance and national crisis, seeking God's guidance for their people (Jeremiah 36:9, Ezra 8:21-23). Even in the New Testament, Paul, one of the most influential writers of the Bible, fasted after encountering Jesus on the road to Damascus (Acts 9:9), marking a pivotal transformation in his life and ministry. Peter received divine revelation about the inclusion of the Gentiles into God's kingdom while fasting and praying (Acts 10:9-10).

The Bible was not written by ordinary men with mere human understanding; it was crafted through the hands of those who humbled themselves before God, fasting and seeking revelation. They didn't rely on their intellect alone but positioned themselves spiritually to hear and record the word of God. When we read Scripture, we are not simply reading history—we are engaging with the living, breathing revelation of God, given to those who earnestly sought Him through sacrifice and devotion.

I want to reemphasize; **fasting is the process of extraction in the spirit.** It removes the unreacted and impure areas of your life to keep just the essentials so that your predestined image can live thus making you more valuable. You picked up this book because you are ready to meet the better version of yourself.

Revealing the Original You

Let me give you a little glimpse. The Bible tells us that when God created the heavens and the earth, He saw it and said, "*This is good.*" I can imagine Him nodding His head as He expressed His delight.

Then, God said, "*Let the earth sprout vegetation, all kinds of trees that grow seed-bearing fruit so that these seeds can produce more plants and trees according to their kind.*" God saw this and nodded, "*This is good.*"

Then God said, "*Let lights appear in the sky,*" and it happened. The larger light was meant to govern the day, and the smaller light to govern the night. He saw this and nodded, "*This is good.*"

Have you ever stopped to think about the power the sun holds? Just trying to look at it is painful. It's a massive ball of fire that holds the power to light the whole earth.

I've seen power plants around our city. These power plants carry a lot of energy—enough to keep the lights on in the town. But when I talk about the sun, I'm not talking about lighting up a town, a region, a state, or even a country—not even a continent or hemisphere. I'm talking about the entire planet. The most important source of light, heat, and energy on this earth is the sun.

I get it now. I understand why God said, *"This is good."*

And just like that, God created everything with His words: the sky, the waters, the beasts of the earth, and the ocean. But when it came to man, the Bible tells us that **God created man**. I repeat, He created man from the dust of the ground. In this case, He didn't speak man into existence—He formed him out of clay. God needed to be intentional with humanity.

He made them male and female in His likeness and image. In other words, He made a being just like Himself: God.

What comes next is the first blessing. God saw them, blessed them, and declared, *"Be fruitful and multiply. Fill the earth and govern it. Reign over all creation."*

As God looked at man this time, He said, *"This is **very** good."*

Your original self was created to be like God. You were handmade by the Master Craftsman to reflect Him. To create with your words, just like your Father. To multiply and expand.

There was a seed of greatness implanted within you so that you could give birth to it. This seed was meant to lead you to dominate and radiate His glory, just like the sun radiates its light.

Hebrews 1:3 (NLV) says, *"The Son radiates God's own glory and expresses the very character of God, and He sustains everything by the mighty power of His command."*

This was humanity's original identity. But sin tampered with us, making us opaque. We stopped shining, our authority was stripped away, and our original identity was hidden behind lies.

Most of humanity operates under a false identity. Most of humanity works below its true power.

Let's take this a little deeper. I heard this from Dr. Myles Munroe, and it blew my mind.

Why do you think God put Adam to sleep when He extracted Eve out of him?

God designed man with the ability to create, reflecting His own divine nature. However, when it came to forming Eve, this was a work God intended to do alone. The Bible tells us that God caused Adam to fall into a deep sleep, and perhaps this was to ensure that Adam would fully trust in God's process rather than attempt to take matters into his own hands. Just as sons naturally desire to imitate their fathers, we, as God's creation, long to reflect Him. Yet, some aspects of creation—especially giving life—belong to God alone.

Something interesting to note is that when extraction occurs, it hurts—it causes pain. God put Adam to sleep and performed the first surgery. With the right dosage of anesthesia, God took a rib out of Adam and closed the opening. It was from that rib that God made woman.

And why am I telling you all this?

Because, like the rib, what is valuable must be extracted. And like fasting, extraction hurts. But the result reveals the path to true wealth.

To state the fact: yes, I did cover Genesis, and that was to show you the original you.

A Call to Action

This book is for those who are tired of merely surviving. It's for those who are ready to thrive and leave a lasting impact. You were created to produce fruit that carries weight and transforms lives. Don't underestimate the power within you. Like the seed, your potential is limitless when nurtured in the right environment.

Are you ready to rediscover your potential?

Are you ready to embrace the discipline of fasting and unlock the essence of the Holy Spirit within you?

If so, let's continue this journey together and step into the abundant life you were created to live.

2

The Hard Truth

"Fasting is the joy of sharing with the poor. It is not just giving up food, but sharing with those who have nothing." —Mother Teresa of Calcutta

From personal experience, I can tell you that I give birth to something new every time I fast. So, I decided to tag every fast with a new petition. If my petition pleases God, glory to Him. If it does not, He lets me know. It's easier for me to accept His "*no*" when I fast. I can testify; He never misses an opportunity to outdo Himself.

In my last book, I shared with you the vision of the local church I pastor. In January of 2021, we moved into our new location. We had talked about moving to the city for years. We had discussed finding a new place we could call home, and guess what? It materialized. God provided everything—from the location to the plans, the finances, the right people, and the final touches. I'm telling you; God is never shorthanded. We've been in our new location for four years now, and I repeat, **God has been the provider of it all.**

You want to know something I noticed? I asked God for a new home for our church before I asked Him for a home for my family and me. What's crazy is that I didn't have a place I could call my own, but I was working towards building a place our community could call their church home. This might not fit your mental construct, but please bear with me.

Humans are naturally egocentric. We think about ourselves—our desires, our wants, our needs—before we think about others' desires, wants, and needs. This became the new norm after the fall. We might not say it, but our lifestyle spits it out.

You picked up this book because you are ready to expose certain areas within you that have hindered your true self from living. When the light exposes what is hidden, then you can be intentional with the change. The lack of knowledge keeps you, but wisdom releases you. In other words, not knowing what is holding you back will continue holding you back.

The lack of knowledge keeps you, but wisdom releases you.

Going back to the year we moved into our new location; I did my second 21-day juice fast. I tagged it with a prayer for a new home for my family. You might not believe it, but that same year, in April—just three months after my fast—God gave us our first home. And you want to know something? I was stress-free throughout the whole process.

For those of you who have purchased a home, you know that it can be extremely stressful. The whole application process, the documents you must submit—check stubs, tax returns from the last two years, your credit score, and the down payment—can take a toll. When you are finally approved, the bank sets a closing date. If you're a beginner, you're so excited for that day, but if you're like me, you aren't celebrating yet.

You might be confused because I said this was the first home I purchased for myself. That is true. I learned about the housing market, buying, and selling because my father has been in this business for over 30 years. Growing up, we saw this time and time again. As the seller, you have payment deadlines, and everyone involved in the construction of the home wants their money. It can get very stressful if you don't prepare ahead of time. Growing up, our home felt it.

For the most part, the first closing day is never final; it gets postponed a few times until everything is set. While this is happening, if you are the buyer and are buying through a bank loan, you need to make sure your credit score does not change. If it does, that can ruin your entire application process. You could have a big setback or, worse, get denied.

When we started the application process for the purchase of our home, the first thing we did was place our trust in God. To be honest with you, from day one, it was all a very smooth process. I trusted, without a doubt. **Self-doubt? Out!** If the home was for us, then God would make it happen, and if it wasn't for us, we weren't going to force anything.

The good news is that it was for us. God made it happen, and it was such a quick and simple process. We went through it with a very unique filter: trust. Everything is much easier when you trust.

We may not have the newest house or the prettiest *home*, but it's the perfect place for us. My favorite part of this particular season was trusting God 100%. It's not enough to say that you trust God; you must live like you trust Him. So, how did we acquire this trust? What did we do to lay our hearts and minds on it? I like to call it *"the fast mode."* That fast made our doubts and insecurities so small that they no longer hindered our lives. That fast literally made everything faster and smoother for us. We stopped wasting our time on things we had no control over. This reminds me of a scripture we studied in our last empowerment session. Jesus declared:

"That is why I tell you not to worry about everyday life, whether you have enough food and drink, or enough clothes to wear. Isn't life more than food, and your body more than clothing? Look at the birds. They don't plant or harvest or store food in barns, for your heavenly Father feeds them. And aren't you far more valuable to Him than they are? Can all your worries add a single moment to your life?" (Matthew 6:25-27 NLT)

You know, at times we think that it's taking too long to see the hand of God work in our favor. At times, we feel discouraged and question God: *"When is it going to be my turn?"* You see everyone making it. Everyone is achieving and acquiring, and it just seems like your time will never come.

Pablo and I had been married for 15 years, and we still hadn't purchased our own home. You would imagine by this time we should have already gone through a couple. Well, technically, we did go through a couple of homes, but sadly, they were not ours. The first few years we lived with my father-in-law. To be honest with you, I wouldn't change it for the world. My father-in-law became my best friend. He definitely showed me a unique kind of love I had never experienced. In the latter years, we lived in my parents' home.

Both places poured into us. Both places helped us mature in certain areas of our lives. For instance, my parents' house taught me how to cut grass. LOL, no, really, it did. They have a big property—eight acres full of mature trees with a lake on one side. Having a ranch is beautiful, but it sure is a lot of work. Both homes prepared us for the moment we would have our own. You see, it wasn't that God was taking forever; it was that it took us a while to be ready for it. Our character had to be trained and molded so that we would be able to cultivate the spirit of a home. Our home needed to be purpose-driven. We needed to learn how to serve and do it with a willing heart. I am grateful to God that He gave us the opportunity to serve my parents and my father-in-law in their different seasons.

Our home needed to be purpose-driven. We currently have a waterfront property a little under an acre. More good news: I don't have to cut much grass. It's been three years now, and I can tell you I like my house, but most of all, I love my home. This 21-day fast was tagged my *temporary affliction*. It was a sacrifice that had a great return.

The Threshing Floor

I want to say fasting is like the threshing floor for the farmer. The threshing floor is a place of separation. After the harvest is picked up, it gets taken here so that the good grain can be separated from the useless straw. The threshing floor is a place of exposure. It all seems good when it is picked, but not all of it is useful. At times, the stalk and other parts of the plant get thrown in with the seed. Don't get me wrong—every part of the plant is important, but not all gives profit.

Every part of the plant is important, but not all gives profit.

There's a verse in the Bible that describes just this:

"All things are permitted, but not all things are profitable. All things are permitted, but not all things build up." (1 Corinthians 10:23 LEB Version)

When it's time to distribute the best product, you must collect the most valuable part of the crop.

Fasting exposes those areas of your life that have been taking your value. It allows you to see what was beneficial for the season but is no longer needed. Fasting gives you the ability to distinguish those areas that build you up from those that tear you down.

Closet Equals Identity

It's crazy to say this, but at times, our greatest enemy isn't our rival. Our biggest enemy is ourselves. We both build and destroy that which took sacrifice, time, money, and effort. It doesn't make sense, but that is the reality.

I was talking to my sister on the phone today, and I was telling her that my mom came over and helped me rearrange my living room. It looks more spacious, and it feels so good to have it nice and clean. I told her, *"Now I just need to clean my room and my office. Man, everything is so out of order,"* which led me to say, *"Imagine how my heart is."* Don't judge me—ask yourself the same question. Ponder upon it. The truth is our lifestyle reveals our hearts.

The truth is our lifestyle reveals our hearts.

She mentioned, *"Man, I need to clean my closet. I always have the hardest time cleaning it."* *"Our closet represents our identity,"* I added.

Wow, that hit us both! Both statements were the mere truth. We have the hardest time acknowledging and cleaning out ourselves. We say there is nothing wrong with us, but is that the truth? Look inside your closet. Maybe it is organized. Maybe it is clean, but let's dive in here.

It may get uncomfortable. There is nothing comfortable about fasting. It's a time of confrontation and change. Who likes to be confronted? Who likes change? There are some brave ones that raise their hands right away. Well, that's not me.

Do you have clothes in your closet that no longer fit you, and you keep telling yourself you're going to fit into them one day? Are there any clothes in your closet that you have never worn and still have tags on them? Are there any clothes in your closet that you overused and no longer use, but you keep telling yourself, "What if I need it?" Are there any clothes in your closet that are out of style, but you believe they will eventually come back into style?

Once again, I tell you, our closet describes our identity. Our closet reveals our heart. It shows us a picture of our mind. Our closet gives us a list of our mental inventory. For some, it can be a waste of space. For others, it can be overloaded. A clean, organized closet filled with only the useful items can definitely help your true self materialize. It will remove doubt and insecurity. You won't waste time, and the time that you do have can be used for opportunities.

If you want to get to know someone and take your relationship more seriously, ask them if you can take a look in their closet. If they hesitate, you will know why. **Our closet reveals our heart. It shows us a picture of our mind.**

Fasting is like closet cleaning. It helps you remove the unnecessary items taking up space in your life. It helps you declutter your mind and organize your heart. It sets you up to have a great day every day.

Facing the Mess

It's not enough to know there is a problem. So many of us have built our relationships on problems upon problems. We don't stop to confront or face the situation because we know it will get uncomfortable. Who likes confrontation, anyways? We create a habit of overlooking things and moving on. We tell ourselves, "*No pasa nada,*" which means "*it's okay.*" The result ends up as a heap of problems. This shows up as divorce in marriages, bankruptcy in business, the student loan crisis in the educational system, and full prisons in the criminal justice system. A bit extreme, right? Well, these are just a few.

Having the knowledge is not enough. Knowing that your closet is a mess will not magically organize itself. You will have to be intentional about making this change. The sooner you face the problem, the sooner you can make the decision to cause this transformation. It will take time and effort. It might be uncomfortable. At this point, you cannot excuse yourself; you are way past accepting the problem. Don't go back to playing the blame game. Accepting responsibility will ease the process.

Now, let's go past the organization and closet cleaning. Maybe you have done this plenty of times. My next question would be: how long does it remain organized? Sometimes, it doesn't even take a day until it looks like you didn't do anything to it, or you see an empty space and feel it needs to get filled. The result is a closet full of nothing to wear.

I need you to understand this: adding something new will not solve the underlying issues. The problem that you face today is a result of an issue that you have outstanding. What fasting does is it takes you to the starting point. It helps you unlearn to relearn. It gives you the sound mind to break bad habits and start training in new ones. You begin to value what you didn't value, and it becomes a part of your new lifestyle.

What's Blocking You?

In Luke 19, Zacchaeus, a wealthy and corrupt tax collector, had lived a life full of worldly success but was spiritually bankrupt. He was aware that something within him was blocking the deeper blessings he longed for, but it wasn't until he encountered Jesus that he faced the truth.

Jesus called Zacchaeus down from the tree, and in that moment, Zacchaeus recognized what had been preventing him from living fully: his greed and dishonesty. He didn't just acknowledge the problem; he took action. He vowed to give half of his wealth to the poor and pay back four times what he had taken. This moment of self-awareness and action was his breakthrough.

Fasting works in much the same way. It forces us to slow down and confront the areas in our lives that are preventing us from receiving God's full blessing. Just as Zacchaeus faced his internal blockage head-on, fasting allows us to expose and deal with the hidden parts of ourselves that may be hindering our growth. When we fast, we give God the opportunity to reveal what needs to change, and to choose to take action once we know the truth. Through fasting, we invite God to reveal these blocks and help us overcome them, leading to greater change and blessing. Fasting isn't just about abstaining from food; it's about allowing God to shine a light on those areas in our lives that need transformation.

Fasting isn't just about abstaining from food; it's about allowing God to shine a light on those areas in our lives that need transformation.

Call to Action

Now it's your turn; take a moment to reflect on the areas in your life that may be holding you back. What are the *"cluttered closets"* in your heart and mind? What fears, doubts, or past experiences are taking up space and preventing you from stepping into the life you're meant to live?

I challenge you to take a step of faith. Whether it's through fasting, prayer, or simply a commitment to trust in God fully, make a decision today to begin the process of decluttering your heart. Allow Him to expose what's been hidden and give you the wisdom to let go of what no longer serves your purpose.

Remember, transformation begins when you are intentional. It's not enough to acknowledge the mess – it's time to clean the house, both in your mind and in your spirit. What's one thing you can do this week to start this process? Start small, stay consistent, and watch as God leads you to a life of greater purpose, peace, and trust.

Remember, transformation begins when you are intentional.

3

Discovering Your Treasure

"Do you wish your prayer to
fly toward God? Give it two
wings: fasting and almsgiv-
ing." —St. Augustine

Hidden treasures are meant to be discovered. Just like the
discipline and determination within humankind, we
can find other levels of treasure. Fasting has been instrumental
in unveiling these hidden gems, allowing us to unearth our
unique strengths.

For athletes, it can pave the way to unparalleled success, while
entrepreneurs can harness innovation and creativity for ground-
breaking ventures and business growth. Fasting serves as a mecha-

nism for personal discovery, enabling individuals to realign, reset, and prepare for unprecedented growth.

So, what does this mean? I remember when the New Year was about to start. Of course, we all wanted to finish strong, but once again, I was exhausted. I needed to realign myself. I was working too hard and not producing enough. I needed to recalibrate.

I could relate this to my car. I noticed, while driving, that one of my shoulders and arms was feeling a lot of stress. It felt tight and very tiring. This is something my husband would call "*mouse neck*." It's the tension in your shoulder caused by using the mouse when working in an office.

What was happening to me was that I had started holding onto the wheel much tighter because the car was trying to drive itself out of the lane. I realized that the tires needed to be aligned. I had been doing this for months, exerting more energy and strength when the problem could have been fixed with a quick stop at a tire shop.

This is exactly what happens to us in the second part of each year. To be honest, I think we just need a tire rotation on our priorities. We need to take a moment to realign our actions so that they run in the same direction as our priorities and don't find themselves fighting against each other.

To be honest, I think we just need a tire rotation on our priorities.

I needed a fast, and I needed it quickly. The New Year was about to start, and I was ready for a reset. I took it seriously. I needed to give birth to something new. My prayer was tagged with, "I want to want You more." That was my desire—I just wanted the person of Jesus.

Now, let me explain. Some people believe Jesus was a great prophet. Others believe He was a great teacher. Most Christians would call Him the Savior of the world, while others don't even believe He existed. Let me explain who Jesus is to me.

Jesus is my Savior. When I had no name, He gave me one. The moment I met Jesus, things changed. He gave me purpose and hope to believe there was something greater out there for me. Jesus accepted me when I felt like a reject. He spoke to me in a way no one had ever talked to me. He made me feel loved and important.

You might ask, *"How did you hear His voice?"*

It wasn't audible. Let me go deeper. Change occurs when you encounter the person of Jesus. Jesus is a revolutionary. He doesn't leave you the same. If He did, then there would be no point in Him meeting you. Transformation occurs. You finally feel alive, with a sense of direction. You stop existing, and you begin to live. Jesus knows you by name. Sometimes, it's easy for people to miss you, but not Jesus. There is a space in His heart reserved just for you.

Once you encounter Him, you will understand what I'm saying. So, my petition during this fast was that I wanted to grow in passion, in love, more and more with Jesus. I didn't want to be comfortable with the portion of Jesus that I knew. I wanted a fresh revelation—a closer look at Him.

I concluded my fast, and it was a success. There was a craving inside of me that I couldn't satisfy. I woke up wanting more and more. My moments with Jesus became more intimate. I remember starting to write immediately. I began documenting moments of my life, typing my encounters and my conversations with God. Before I knew it, there was a book manifesting. A book? Yes, there was a book being born. Coral writing a book? Yes. I didn't even like to read; much less think I could write my own. Let me tell you—I was mediocre when it came to reading. I would start a book and never finish it.

Overcoming Barriers

That year, I gave birth to my first book. It literally took nine months to write and finalize. I couldn't believe it. I wasn't smart enough to be an author. I wasn't smart enough to put something together and publish it.

But I remember speaking this out to the universe, and my father-in-law is my witness. I told him, *"One day, I'm going to publish my own book, and you will be my accountability partner."* I asked him to sign my journal, and he dated it March 21, 2011. That day, I sowed a seed of faith, hoping it would come to life.

"One day, I'm going to publish my own book, and you will be my accountability partner."

Signature: Pedro Aguilar 3-21-11

My life with Jesus took a complete turn back in 2009, when I said *"I do"* to Jesus. I committed myself to cultivating a healthy relationship with Him. I wanted to get to know the God who saved me. I had enough with learning about the God my grandmother served, and the God my mother knew. I was ready to meet the God who loved me. That being said, I adopted new habits. I started reading. But not just that—I developed a passion for reading. I started collecting books, and every conference I attended, I was intentional about buying new ones, whether they were spiritual or based on leadership.

I remember walking into my brother's office. His bookshelf caught my attention. He had about ten books at that time. I was inspired by him to start my own collection. *"That's all it took to inspire you?"* you may ask. The answer is **yes**. You see, my brother graduated last in his class. He was dyslexic. He didn't like to read—actually, he couldn't read. So, for him to have a library, that meant he had tapped into a season of transformation, just like the butterfly. The cocoon was stuck with no progress, until he stepped into his season of change.

Without him even knowing it, he was about to hit the jackpot. Why do I tell you this? My brother is one of the best communicators I know. He's impressive when it comes to public speaking. He has a gift for transforming the poorest, coldest environment into something rich. He unlocks the gifts trapped inside of people.

He consistently quotes Dr. Myles Monroe, who said, *"The wealthiest place on earth is the cemetery because underneath that dirt are infinite amounts of books, inventions, ideas, songs, businesses that were never born."* That real estate consists of a wealth of potential that could have been, but never was.

The Millionaire Fast

Now, do you understand the concept of the millionaire fast?

A few years after I said yes to Jesus, I spoke it out: "One day, I'm going to write my own book." I said it, but I'm not sure I believed it 100%. I released it, though. That was my first step. It started with a thought and a declaration.

Going back to the results of that fast, that year, I gave birth to my first book. Isn't it crazy? What's crazier is that I wrote that book during the pandemic. What paralyzed most people stirred up my spirit to bring forth a dream that had been inside of me this whole time. Maybe you've never dreamed of writing your own book but let me tell you—what seems impossible is only impossible for the person who has no faith. I want to inspire you to make a mindset shift. Don't see the problem—grasp the opportunity.

Don't see the problem—grasp the opportunity.

Crisis can either paralyze you or catapult you. What makes the difference? It's character. During the pandemic, many turned to comfort in different ways—some found escape in food or binge-watching shows, simply trying to cope with an uncertain world. I completely understand that response because hard times affect us all differently. For me, things unfolded another way. There was sickness, but also healing. There was fear, but also hope. While isolation kept many apart, my home remained full. The cup felt empty, yet it was preparing to overflow. The world was on pause, but my heart was moving.

We all had the same opportunity but made different choices. You can say, "*Well Coral you didn't lose a loved one. Maybe you had no one sick.*" Let me correct you. I did lose a loved one, my second father which was my father-in-law. I also went through the trauma of my dad being at the verge of death, hospitalized for over 40 days. We were not allowed to see him. I go in-depth on this season in my *Book Self-Doubt Out! God's Masterpiece* —I wrote that book when it was actually happening.

Instead, I chose to write down my moments, my encounters with God. I documented the process because I knew that hope would come in the morning.

I chose to take crisis and make it my opportunity.

Let me speak some truth to you:

Everyone is capable. There's no question about that. There's a reason why there are moments when you lay awake at night, dreaming of what could be. Maybe your dream is different from mine. It might not be a book, but a composition or a song. Perhaps your dream is a business or building a school—creating something that will change the lives of humanity. If this dream is inside of you, it's because someone greater than you placed it there. Let me be honest with you: This dream isn't even about you; it's about the Creator who chose you. He gave it to you because He knows that you can.

Your job is to believe it, activate it, and extract it!

This is the reason I chose to write this book. There are so many hidden treasures within you that you have not discovered yet. You must be intentional with God so that He can show you the way to the hidden wells of wisdom and creativity you own. These treasures are no secret to God. Our job on this earth is to discover these riches and enrich this land with them. These riches point back to the person of Jesus who wants to abide in you.

**There are so many hidden treasures within
you that you have not discovered yet.**

You know how I told you, when you encounter Jesus, He changes you. There is something about His Spirit and the essence of God inside of you that, when they make contact with each other, the supernatural occurs. Fasting moves you from a natural lifestyle to a supernatural life.

Unlocking Your Body's Secrets

Physically, fasting delivers you from sickness and infirmities. An article I came across titled *8 Health Benefits of Fasting, Backed by Science* explains that fasting can offer numerous health advantages, such as aiding in weight loss, improving blood sugar levels, and potentially protecting against medical conditions like cancer and neurodegenerative diseases.

Fasting helps your body rejuvenate. There are hormones in your body called ketones that are produced when you fast. These hormones have a specific purpose: they speak life to your body! They reconstruct damaged tissue. It seems as if it turns a switch in your body, and you begin to age backward. I know that's a bold statement, and yet a bit exaggerated, what I mean is that you begin to look younger and feel healthier. When you fast, you tap into a part of yourself you didn't even know existed.

Fasting stimulates the body to release ketones, an "anti-aging" molecule that serves as an alternative energy source when glucose is unavailable. Research indicates that ketones help rejuvenate blood vessels by promoting the regeneration of their interior cells, which can slow down the aging process.

I'm not claiming to be an expert in biology or chemistry, but through researching for this book, I discovered something remarkable: the human body was designed to sustain and renew itself, and fasting plays a vital role in that process.

Put simply:

- **Ketones** act like a guardian fuel, sparing glucose while boosting the rejuvenating NAD^+ current in the brain.

- **Organ pruning & stem-cell bloom** follow each prolonged fast, rebuilding tissues with fresher parts.

- **Hormonal re-tuning** (lower IGF-1, higher IGFBP-1) flips the cellular mindset from relentless growth to diligent maintenance.

Fasting isn't deprivation, it's strategic renovation. A brief retreat that allows the body to return stronger, leaner, and, in many ways, younger.

You tap into a part of yourself you didn't even know existed.

Unlocking Your Dreams

Let's go back to the dreams. You know how I told you that God is the one who deposits these dreams in us. We are all born with these dreams—some more than others—and they all vary. They are unique.

Let's talk about the first man, for instance. The Bible tells us God created Adam from the dust of the ground, and He blew His breath into his nostrils and made him a living soul. When God gave Adam his first job, God knew Adam would be successful. God made him capable. The Bible tells us Adam named all the animals. Where do you think Adam got these names from? They were found within.

Now let's go deeper. The Bible tells us that when God saw Adam alone, He said, *This is not good. I am going to make him a helpmeet.* Like I explained in Chapter 1, God gave Adam the best anesthetic, and he fell asleep. The Bible tells us God extracted a rib out of Adam, and He made the woman. When Adam finally arose from his sleep, he saw the woman, and he said, *"Wow, God, You're good. This is really good."* Of course, this is what I believe Adam responded; these aren't exact words from the Bible.

Let me make something clear. When God made man, He created him from the dust of the ground, but when He made woman, He extracted her out of the man. In other words, Adam carried Eve within him since the moment God made him. The dream was inside of him. Not sure exactly how long Adam lived alone, but the moment arrived that the maturity date of that dream was up. It was time to materialize.

Just like Adam carried this dream, Eve also carried God's dream: she would be the mother of all living. Maybe you don't believe the Bible. At least take it as a story and understand the principle. When we were sent to planet Earth, we were sent with a hidden treasure, with a special essence. We are not meant to die with this essence. Our job on this Earth is to discover it and make the Earth richer with it. It must live, not get trapped in a cemetery.

Even though fasting is not the only way, it is a vehicle that can lead you to discover the treasures of greatness hidden within you.

In this particular year, God allowed me to give birth to my first book and to start the process of our church relocation. I say *first* because I am currently writing my second book, and I am a witness that there are more books within me that are ready to be created. At times, you may feel accomplished and happy with the level of success you've reached, but God always surprises you with more.

Call to Action:

Take a moment now to reflect on what treasures lie within you. What dreams have you tucked away, believing they were impossible? Just as I discovered my calling through fasting and personal accountability, you can too. Begin today by making space for God to reveal the hidden gems in your life. Start small—commit to seeking Him through prayer, fasting, and dedication. Watch as He unlocks your preset abilities. You're ready for what's inside you to come to life.

4

Waiting Is Not Popular

"The best way to find yourself is to lose yourself in
the service of others. Fasting is a way of aligning
body, mind, and spirit in that service." Mahatma
Gandhi

You're probably going to say, "*Another one Coral?*" Yes!
Another one!

You know how there are some people that you meet that their
story just keeps getting worse and worse. Well in this case it just
keeps getting better and better.

This book isn't another news story. This book is about the
good news. I believe you have had your portion of bad news,
it's about time you picked up a book that would inspire you to
step out of the box and explore the beauty life has for you.

I preached a series called Step Out of The Box last month. God was really tugging at my heart. He spoke to me about the comfort zone and about these systems we have adopted that have kept us from seeing all that we are created to do.

When we talk about leadership, the comfort zone is not a place to inhabit. Leaders are not formed in this zone. There is no growth. There is no change. Everything is constant and expected. You can forecast and hit the mark every time.

The comfort zone is a dangerous place for humanity. Humanity was meant to thrive, to grow, to create. Creativity dies in comfort. It is no place for a dreamer. It is no place for someone who practices fasting. Fasting is uncomfortable! **Emphasis Added**!

I don't know why God made me this way but when he knit me together in my mother's womb, he placed a challenge default setting in me. This button goes off every year at least once but sometimes thrice. LOL I always have to challenge myself. It hurts. It's painful but I love it. It's like the Cross fitters, we pay to die every day. We pay to get beat up, but we love it and can't live without it.

So, it's about to be the New Year. Again, my inner coach tells me: *In order to have what you've never had, you must do what you've never done.*

Who's my inner coach? The Holy Spirit.

What challenge will I take up now? The New Year fast was about to start. Would this be my third-year juicing? I started getting bombarded with thoughts: *You've done this before. It must hurt. It needs to feel like a sacrifice.* I felt God stirring my spirit to do a complete fast—a water fast.

This would be my first time doing a 21-day water fast. I had heard about people doing this, but no one close to me. Dr. Myles Munroe would practice this fast on any normal year. And he survived. So that means I would survive too.

I took the challenge, and I said, "*Yes Lord. Let's do it. But I don't just want to starve myself; I need to be intentional about my experience with you.*"

I decided to separate myself for the 21 days. I would be fasting all food and would be drinking only water. I felt healthy and I was at my fittest, so I saw nothing really keeping me back from being able to accomplish this goal.

What do I mean by separating myself? I disconnected myself from everything. I am a pastor, and my job is to preach and be present at church. These 21 days I wasn't a pastor. I was just a child in need of her father. I didn't go to church. I didn't preach. I didn't leave my house. I didn't go to the gym. I didn't get on social media.

I literally stayed home for three weeks. If I was going to do something, I was going to give it my best. Jesus deserved my best. He needed all of me—not just part of me. Let me tell you. I got what I wanted and much more.

Jesus deserved my best. He needed all of me—not just part of me.

The Experience

This is crazy! Where do I start? I was hungry. I was starving. I know you might be saying duh!

The first days I felt stuck. Nothing was happening. I felt numb, deaf, blind and mute. When I fast first of all it is for spiritual reasons, what comes after is secondary. I don't fast to lose weight. I know that's trendy, but if you approach it through the principle, I am teaching you in this book, you will lose weight and become the richest person on earth. Hence the Millionaire Fast.

So anyways, the first day passed and I felt nothing. The second day went by, and I heard nothing. The third day arrived, and I saw nothing.

Was there something wrong with me? Was my motive selfish? Was there pride? I understand that pride and the ego are repellants to the presence of God. Why couldn't I hear God?

Something you will notice when you fast is that you become very sensitive. You get very emotional. God begins to release you from trapped emotions—emotions that you might have not realized needed to be treated.

When I fast, I'm intentional about worship. I set up my whole playlist to create an atmosphere of brokenness and humility. In essence, that's exactly what a fast is. It's not a time to celebrate or party. It's a time of mourning and surrender, a time of repentance and forgiveness, a time to analyze your life and put order to things that are out of order.

I was stuck. I didn't know what to pray. I didn't know what to say. I don't know if you have ever felt like this before, but this was not good. I didn't feel good. I'm a crier. This is a way I find deliverance. It wasn't until the fourth day that I saw my breakthrough.

As I started the fast, I felt I was good overall. I was a good wife, a good daughter, a good mother, a good pastor, and a good friend. It was not until the moment I was lying on my bed, face down on that fourth day, that I felt a great conviction fill my heart. I realized I wasn't as good as I thought.

I had been failing as a sister. My relationship with one of my brothers was completely broken. We had been so close, serving alongside each other for almost a decade, and now it had been five years since we went our separate ways.

I knew I was failing as a daughter. Every time I heard something I didn't like, I would snap, and without thinking, I would disrespect my parents, especially my dad. We bumped heads a lot. I was prideful and thought I had the right to.

I started asking myself, how much time do you make for your brothers and sister? How often do you invite them to eat at your house? How often do you serve them? How often do you interrupt your agenda just to love on them? The answer was hardly ever.

I started thinking about my role as a wife. In the beginning I would cook for my husband every day but as of lately I would excuse myself. I was good but that is not the wife I wanted to be. I wanted to be great.

I thought about my role as a mother. I was failing my daughter. Last year, my oldest had the hardest time believing in herself. Her self-esteem was wasted; her self-confidence was on the floor. She had gained so much weight, and we didn't understand why.

To be honest with you, she has always practiced a healthy diet. She even went vegetarian for a whole year when she was eleven years old. She did this on her own. I didn't ask her to—it wasn't my idea. I am a meat eater at heart!

I remember she cried to me, and it broke my heart because I didn't know how to help her. That summer, I ended up taking her to a specialist, and it turned out her thyroid was all messed up.

The Revelation

The point is God began to reveal those areas of my life where I had been failing. The whole time I thought I was okay. From the fourth day forward, I cried every day. It was a healthy type of guilt I felt because it was helping me cut ties with those bad habits and bad systems I had adopted.

Those 21 days were intentional. I read a lot; six books in 3 weeks. I read the New Testament. I heard numerous preaching's. I found new worship songs. There was a new melody playing in my heart. That is what I needed. I needed a fresh wind. A rekindled passion. I needed my heart to be in tune with God's heart and I was finally getting there.

My prayer in this fast was simply I want you, Lord. I will wait for you until you finish the work you have started in my life. I didn't want to stay comfortable getting by with good. I wanted to give God and everyone around me great. They deserved nothing less.

It was one cold morning when I stepped outside before the sun had even risen. I was all wrapped up in my cover on my knees by the Resaca, telling God, "*Aqui te esperare*," which means I will wait for you here. I am not going anywhere. I will wait.

The hardest thing to do at times is wait. Because of the culture and the environment, we live in, waiting is not popular. We want everything now and as quickly as possible. But I was convinced and with a faith filled heart, I repeated, "I will wait for you here Lord." What I wanted was to experience God in a way I had never experienced him before. When I opened my eyes after that beautiful time of surrender, the sun was completely risen.

I lost track of time, but time didn't matter anyways. I had nothing else to do. My agenda had been separated to do just this. My nights were pretty long. I couldn't really sleep. I was alert and ready to go. When I did sleep though, I had nightmares. My nightmares were about food. One night I dreamed that I was at the drive through ordering pizza but before I went to pay, I remembered, "I can't eat this. I'm fasting." When I woke up, I felt relieved. It was just a dream.

Another dream I had was that we were at church, and we were feeding families. We served everyone nachos. The line finally finished, and it was our turn to eat. When I was about to serve myself, the food ran out. I woke up shortly after. That dream really hurt. I really did want some nachos. My greatest enemy during that fast was not when I was awake but when I was asleep.

During the day I felt strong. I cooked for my family every day and honestly, I was good. I didn't feel tempted. It is no lie. Those three weeks I not only had a spiritual cleanse, but I also had the time to clean my house. One of the rooms in my house has a lot of windows. In my opinion it's the room with the best view which leads to the Resaca. So, I even had the chance to clean my windows from the outside and the inside. I thought the view was pretty clear. It wasn't until I cleaned the windows that I realized the view had actually been very cloudy.

This is our perspective of life at times. We think we're pretty good, pretty clean until we stop to really analyze our present state. Is this really excellence or am I just doing enough to be "good"?

My time was about finished. I had completed my 21 days. I thought to myself, maybe I should continue. I've come this far. I can do another 20. Maybe you're getting annoyed by me. This chick is never satisfied. It really was a bittersweet moment. I didn't want to leave the space I had created for Jesus and me. I had never spent so much time with him, and this was quality. 21 days of quality time with my savior. I'm telling you there is nothing that can compare to that genuine moment when you encounter the person of Jesus. It gives you purpose and a reason to live.

My husband did not let me continue the fast so in the evening with the sunset I turned in my fast. Sunsets are always perfect. We think of them as a perfect setting for romance. That's exactly what I experienced with Jesus. It was my love story. It was the renewal of my vows. I drank a little bit of soup, and I enjoyed the moment. I did it. I made it. I felt so much pleasure. It was amazing. I had no regrets.

I took it slow with the food. Every time you do an intense fast with pure water you have to be very careful. You can't just eat like you had never stopped. You can have serious issues if you do not take precautions. You can even lead your heart to stop, and the game is over.

What happens in the next few months is crazy! I still can't even believe it and I am a pretty optimistic person. My husband noticed something different in me. I had lost a lot of weight. Duh! No, seriously! He felt something was different. I didn't feel different other than I felt great. I felt powerful. I felt unstoppable. I was at my healthiest, I was at my fittest physically and spiritually; I was a warrior ready for battle.

I missed a period, but I wasn't a regular, so I didn't think much of it. I told my husband to buy a pregnancy test just in case. We honestly hadn't wasted our money on that anymore. It was always negative anyways. I went to the restroom, did the test and let it set. I still remember it like it was yesterday. We were laying on the bed. All three of us. It was Galilea, my daughter, Pablo, and I. I told Gali, "*You go check. I don't want to look. I don't want to be disappointed again.*" Pablo nodded and said, "*Coral I know already.*" Very calm and convinced he said, "*You're pregnant.*"

Honestly, I didn't feel pregnant. I didn't feel sick. Oh lord! I was sick all day and night for nine months in my first pregnancy with Gali.

Fifteen minutes had already passed. So, I told Gali to go check. She comes back walking into the room with a hunch back and her head tucked into her chest, I ask her Gal, so? Was it positive? She tucked herself in the covers and nodded her head with a smile, yes. *"You're pregnant mom."*

I couldn't believe it. I still can't believe it. Could it be that after **14 years** I could possibly be pregnant? It was so surreal. I stood up and checked it and she was right. It was very clear, "pregnant." My husband just smiled. I did the same. We promised not to say a word to anyone.

That same week I remember my dad sitting me down in his dining table telling me I needed to go to the doctor and get invitro. He strongly believes that if God allowed doctors to find this way of conceiving, then it was okay.

My daughter and I on the other hand, believe that if God really had it in his plans, it would happen the natural way. My dad was very adamant about his advice. He felt I needed to do whatever I could to have more children. By this point I already knew I was pregnant. I was dying on the inside thinking, "If you only knew dad. If you only knew."

A Collective Victory

I believe only two weeks had passed since we had done the pregnancy test. It was a Sunday, and I was preaching. I felt the Holy Spirit tug at my heart. Say the good news. Testify. Share with the church. We had already agreed we were not going to say anything until I was like four months. I couldn't hold it in.

A few weeks prior I was so excited because when it was time to dismiss the kids so they could go to their Sunday school classes, the whole church practically got up. There were a lot of kids. I declared, *"This church is blessed. God's blessing is upon our families. We are being fruitful. There is no doubt about that."* As I spoke that out loud, I said within myself, *"Except your servant Lord."*

So, I started with this. I opened up my heart and was very transparent. I was serious. I told them my story and how I felt. I was fulfilling God's commandment. Very calm and serious I was building the story. I continued, *"And after fourteen years, we are happy to announce to you that we are having a baby."* At that moment it seemed like we had scored the game winning goal! The church erupted with a loud shout. Everyone screamed. The church jumped up and ran towards the altar to congratulate us.

That day we experienced a great victory. It was not only my miracle. That miracle belonged to the whole congregation. There was laughter and tears of joy. God had done it. He surprised us all with a little portion of heaven here on earth.

So, what happened was that my body got a reset with the water fast. I cleansed both spiritually and biologically. I got a fresh start and a new beginning. I finished my fast on the 21st of January 2022 and in February I got pregnant. It literally took nine months to give birth to God's dream. I'm telling there is something about the Spirit of Jesus. It shifts something inside of you and it doesn't let you stay the same.

As soon as His spirit makes contact with His essence in you, it provokes a movement that your body can't contain. The first time around I gave birth to a book in nine months. The second time around I gave birth to my dream, Zerah Judea Aguilar. Why Zerah? It means new beginning and Judea, the praised one. God gave me a new beginning. My story isn't over yet. The praise is barely getting started.

I'm not sure what his dream looks like within you. It may be a book, or a baby, a business, a song, or an invention. It may be something that impacts your family or your community, maybe even your state or your nation, or the entire globe. Whatever the situation may be, this is the time you position yourself in the right place to provoke the birth. You cannot die without witnessing it. Do not steal from humanity. God gave it to you because the world needs it. At the end of the day everything must give glory to God.

I pray, "Make me an answer to my city."

5

My 40-Day Journey

"Some have exalted religious fasting beyond all
Scripture and reason; and others have utterly dis-
regarded it. But fasting, rightly done, brings one
closer to God." —John Wesley

We were getting ready to close out the year. Let me tell
you, my dream had been so tangible, but I still could
not believe it. Even though I felt fatigue and sickness during
the pregnancy, I still couldn't believe it. Every day, I would ask
my husband, *"How did it happen?"* He would say, *"Well, let me
explain."*

I knew how it happened, but why now? Why not ten years ago
or five years ago? What was different this time around? My mind
could not comprehend it. After gaining so much weight, I still
couldn't believe it. After not being able to sleep, I couldn't believe
it. After getting up all night to pee, I still couldn't believe it. I

mean, I knew it was taking place, but I just couldn't believe it had happened.

I know I speak faith, and this might sound pretty negative, but I just couldn't comprehend it. Yet, every time I said, "*I can't believe it*," I always had a smile on my face. It was a joyful moment. My heart laughed, kind of like Sarah, Abraham's wife in the Bible when the angel told her she would have a baby. She was 90 years old!

Let me tell you, my baby was so comfy in mommy's stomach—she did not want to come out. I had to get induced. I was pregnant for over 41 weeks. Elephant or what? Almost. I remember crying at night, telling Pablo, "I just want to meet her already. Why doesn't she want to meet me?"

I was literally in labor for 27 hours. The moment arrived—it was time to push. This chick did not want to leave the comfortable atmosphere God had created for her in my tummy. I was exhausted. I hadn't rested. I hadn't drank water in over 24 hours since I had already been given the anesthetic.

Right before it was time to push, I asked the nurse for some ice. I was dying of thirst. The bad thing is it made things worse. I ended up throwing up. Without having time to catch my breath, the doctor came in. "*It's time.*"

The next moment, I was already pushing. I couldn't hold my breath. I was exhausted even before I started pushing. Without stopping, every ten seconds, I had to push again. After ten minutes of pushing, I couldn't push any longer. I wasn't going to make it.

I remember telling my doctor, "*I can't anymore.*"

She said, "*Yes, you can. If not, I would have done a C-section a long time ago.*"

I attempted a couple more times, and there she was. My dream materialized. It took almost 15 years, but it didn't lie. I was favored, and the word of God did not fail.

Wait for it. It will not lie. Every word that is released out of the mouth of the Father must do what it was sent out to do. "*Wait on the Lord: be of good courage, and he shall strengthen thine heart: wait, I say, on the Lord.*" (Psalm 27:14 KJV)

Many would give everything else the credit but God. I won't. It was all God. He had it planned long ago. The story is much more powerful when the impossible occurs. The story is much more impactful when the unexpected happens. I just needed to believe it.

Zerah Judea was born on November 29, 2022. She was a big baby, weighing 8.5 lbs. The following weeks were blissful. I couldn't sleep, but that didn't bother me much. I was on cloud nine. I had the greatest support system—my husband, all my family, and church friends. Everyone was excited. Zerah was the baby everyone had been praying for. She was definitely needed.

A year prior, in 2021, my father-in-law went to be with the Lord. There was an emptiness in our hearts that needed to be filled with joy and laughter. That was Zerah. Let me tell you how impactful her birth was. I received messages from strangers congratulating us. They had been following our story. Our prayers had become their prayers.

Zerah was so loved. Mail kept coming in from all over the place—gifts, money, and blessings in different forms. Honestly, she had everything she needed before I could buy anything. At eleven months old, she still has baby wipes from the gender reveal party. This goes to show that abundance and unity defined this season.

Zerah is almost a year old, and I still can't believe I have another baby. I know you might say, "*Ya! Get it through your head.*" But you wouldn't understand. For almost a decade, every test was negative.

Now it's four of us, and guess what? I want more! My brother Joe tells me, "*Hurry up, Coral. Do another fast so you can get pregnant again,*" as if it were that easy.

I started writing this book in June 2023. Initially I wanted to write a book on the powerful women of the Bible but instead I took this subject. I noticed I had truly been living a lifestyle of fasting. I realized that I had practically done all the fasts in the Bible. *The Daniel's Fast, the Esther Fast,* water fast, dry fast, fruits and vegetables, juices. I had already lived this book it just needed to be documented.

There was one particular fast, though, I had not attempted: the **40-day water fast**. That was intimidating. My pastor had told me about his experience. It was intense and scary. I always felt like that was impossible. Only superhumans can do something like that.

I had only read about three people doing this fast in the Bible—Jesus, Elijah, and Moses. I never once related to them, nor did I desire to do something like this. Until now.

"*Omg. Again. Why? Why can't you just be normal?*" you may ask.

I don't know. I don't know why God made me this way. Honestly, it's painful, but I love it. I love challenging myself.

This time, I didn't even wait until the new year. I said, "*Normal people wait until the new year. I am not normal. Average people go along with the crowd. I am not average.*" I repeated it once again: *For me to have what I have never had; I must do what I have never done.*

One day, I was talking to my friend Jocelyn, and I told her about my book. I told her, "*I'm writing this book on fasting.*" I explained that the only fast I had not done was the 40-day water fast. I said, "*I'm thinking about it.*" This would be the final piece to my book.

I thought about the pros of finishing this book before the year ended, getting it published, and having it available for the new year. No better time than having this book ready at the beginning of the year. I had one big problem: I was running out of time. October was about to start.

I told her, "*I think I will finish the year with this fast. I'll start November 21 and finish just in time.*"

What she said next challenged me.

"*Why do you have to wait until November? Start now. What's holding you back?*"

I thought about it, and I said, "*Nothing really. You're right. I will. I'll start Oct. 1 after I get back from the trips I already have scheduled.*"

October was truly a busy month. My agenda was full of activity. I had a couple of wedding ceremonies, daily meetings, and coaching sessions. I had just officially launched my own coaching and mentoring business, SDO Coaching Agency. I couldn't postpone my sessions; I was barely gaining momentum. I had to do it. I had already said yes.

So, my journey started on September 30 at 6 p.m. I was in Connecticut. I had been invited to celebrate and minister at the Feast of Tabernacles. I flew in by myself, but I met my brother there. I arrived at midnight Thursday. I spent the morning with my brother dreaming and capturing pictures of the greatest mansions in the U.S. We toured the Vanderbilt Mansion inside and out. It was breathtaking. The house had 50 bedrooms—seventeen were occupied by the family, and the rest were for the servants.

Anyways, even though the view was amazing, I wasn't feeling very well. I hardly got any sleep because my stomach was hurting all night. At dawn, I couldn't hold it any longer. I had to throw up. My body felt weak. My muscles were hurting. My head was throbbing. I had no other choice but to push through the day. I didn't eat much all day except for broth because of my stomachache. I had to be at the tent by 3 p.m. because the sister who had invited me had scheduled me early to give me directions.

Let me share some details.

It was cold and rainy that day. Before I arrived at the tent, I got a message: *"Make sure to stop and buy some rain boots because it is muddy out here."* Well, I'm from Texas—south Texas, to be exact—where the sun and heat are abundant year-round. We don't have winter in the Valley. I was wearing a t-shirt, a sweater, and a coat, but even then, I was still cold.

My brother dropped me off, and there I was—alone, sick, in the cold with a whole bunch of strangers in a strange land. Every hour that passed, I stopped to question myself, "*What am I doing here?*" The night finally ended. I was ready to rest.

The next day I wouldn't preach until 6 p.m., but I was present at the tent by noon. That day, my niece was with me. I didn't feel all that strange anymore.

Evening arrived. As we were worshiping, one of the sisters said, "*Take this time to meditate on the Lord. Allow Him to give you revelation.*" Instantly, God took me to Jesus' experience in the wilderness. The Bible says:

"Then Jesus was led by the Spirit into the wilderness to be tempted by the devil. After fasting forty days and forty nights, he was hungry." (Matthew 4:1-2 NIV)

It was the Spirit that led Jesus into the wilderness. It was the same Spirit that had led me to the wilderness. There was no coincidence that on my first day of fasting, I was in a strange place. I didn't plan it this way. It just happened.

That night, I was able to release the heart of God. There was so much brokenness and humility. I understood it was God all along who had led me there.

The Bible tells us that after Jesus fasted, He was hungry, and angels ministered unto Him. After Jesus left the desert, He stepped into the role of Messiah, the teacher, the Son of the Almighty God. This is when the Son was made manifest. Miracles, signs, and wonders followed Him everywhere He went! Something in Him was activated.

At that moment, I felt hope. I got excited. There was an expectancy in my heart.

I flew back and the challenge began. By the third day, I was dying. Everything was hurting. I asked the Lord; do you think I can really do this?" I heard such a clear response. He said, "*Not by yourself.*" He paused, "*but with me everything is possible.*"

That was my first conversation with God since I had started. It was so clear. I knew when it was him talking even though it sounded like me. You might think I'm crazy but for reals. I could distinguish his tone when he was talking.

This whole season has been about being intentional. I wasn't just going to starve myself. I needed to feed my spirit. I had a whole list of books already lined up to be devoured.

This whole season has been about being intentional.

One of those days while I was praying, I asked the Lord, "*Lord, do you really think I can get pregnant again?*" He responded, "*Why do you want a big family? Are you comparing yourself again to your siblings? I thought we were done with the comparison trap.*"

"*No Lord. It's not that, nor the tax credit for each child,*" I laughed.

"*The more of them I have the more of you I have,*" I responded.

You know how I have been talking to you about the essence that you carry inside of you. Well, this essence is a portion of Jesus. Every time I embrace Galilea, my firstborn it's as if I'm embracing Jesus. Every time I hold Zerah in my arms, it's as if I am holding on to a piece of heaven, my hope.

I told him, *"Lord I want to leave a legacy. I want the virtue and the gifts you have deposited in Pablo and me to continue to pass onto this earth."* I was able to see his expression as he understood what I meant. It was a beautiful and pleasant conversation I had with God that night.

This fast was totally different from the prior years. Number one, this year I had a growing baby to tend to, a new business to care for, a growing church that needed support and to top it off, while I was supposed to be disconnected from the normal church affairs, I had several important phone calls to take care of.

The first was on a Monday. A young woman told me, pastor, God is calling me to another church. That caught me by surprise because all I saw in this young woman was growth. The next day another message came in from another woman from church, pastor I need to talk to you. Another surprise, she was leaving as well. The messages kept arriving. One of them just simply texted that she was leaving for another ministry. Then another person left without even saying anything.

What was happening? Was it a bad time to search for God? Within a matter of two weeks nine people left the church. I don't mean to give you bad news. This really happened.

The great thing about identifying as a child of God is that even bad news in reality is good news. I'll explain later. It's going to get better. I promise.

Let me explain the term **FAST**.

A period of fasting is not a time of celebration, it's a time of testing. You position yourself to get beat up like in CrossFit. Just kidding but for reals. Fasting is a time of pruning. If you want to be that tree that bears a lot of fruit, you will need to prune that tree. At times there are unnecessary branches, dead ones that are just stuck to the tree but are not producing anything.

If your goal is for your tree to grow higher and expand its branches towards the sky, you will need to cut the lower branches that are carrying too much weight. Those branches aren't necessarily bad but for this goal they will not benefit. They need to be clipped off so that the tree can spread.

A gardener knows that the trees need to be pruned yearly so that the harvest can be greater than the prior year. Does it hurt the tree? Yes, but it is a temporary pain for a promising gain.

I understood that our church was being pruned. It is not that the people that left were bad people. It's just that they wouldn't fit the roles in the season we were stepping into. We must understand that certain people, projects, businesses, and even ministries are only for a set time. We need to discern the time we are living in and trust the process.

I was thinking, could have these people waited until I finished my fast? Could they have found a better time to leave? Maybe they thought I was super woman, and it wouldn't hurt me. But come on, I'm only human and I have emotions.

I will be honest though; I understood the time. I respected God's wisdom, and I had peace. Yes, there were people leaving but the church was growing. It might not make sense but that's exactly what happened.

I will repeat what I said earlier, this month of October was about being intentional. I asked the Holy Spirit daily; can we be intentional today. I want you. I'll explain a little more on the Holy Spirit shortly.

I didn't start this fast with a specific petition. I simply told Jesus; I want to document our story. I want to share with the world my moments with you. I am not asking you for anything but everything at the same time. I want you and I know you want me. You want areas of me that I have not surrendered.

I am not asking you for anything but everything at the same time. I want you and I know you want me.

Intentional Reads

I chose books that would lead me to my goal. I read a book on *The Art of War* by Cindy Trimm. It's a book on strategic prayer. Something powerful I learned is that my prayers aren't necessarily bad, but Jesus' prayers are better.

An evangelist shared his testimony that the greatest revivals he ever experienced were when he began to pray Jesus' prayers. Because there is nothing that can compare to the Word—Jesus. When He encounters you, He changes you. Dreams that were long expired take life again. Things that were stuck get loosened. Your spirit gets shaken. Your mind gets unlocked, and you begin to hope where there was no hope. Creativity starts to flow; your faith starts to grow. You begin to see opportunity where all that existed were dead ends and a game over.

I told Jesus during this fast, *I forfeit my prayers. I align my heart, mind, and spirit to pray Your prayers.* I have proven it time and time again: Jesus has better results than me. That's a given.

I also read *Disruptive Thinking* by T.D. Jakes. This book confirmed a series of messages I had preached, which I mentioned in the previous chapter, *Stepping Out of the Box.* Essentially, it's about knowing you were meant for more and breaking out of the systems that have kept you from becoming all God has destined you to be. We get so comfortable doing the same thing. We start believing that what we know is all there is. The opposite is the truth. Just because you don't have knowledge of something doesn't mean it doesn't exist.

I'm totally ready to step out into the unknown to create and discover new ideas, books, songs, businesses, and recipes that are out there for me. I'm ready to grow! Like my sister Lucero said, *I'm ready to blossom.*

Another book I picked up was *The Holy Spirit* by my Pastor Juan De La Garza, and I was also gifted *Host the Holy Ghost* by Vlad

Savchuk. These books motivated me to create an atmosphere for an upper-room experience. The upper room was a historic moment the disciples of Jesus experienced. It was something unique and different. It was supernatural.

The book of Acts tells us that Jesus' disciples were together in the upper room, waiting for a sign. Jesus had told them before He left this earth, *Wait for my gift. I have something special for you. Don't leave this city until the gift arrives.* They didn't have Amazon Prime then, so I think it took 50 days for the gift to arrive.

But when it arrived, OMG, it was out of this world. This gift was worth more than the most beautiful diamond on earth. It was priceless. It didn't look like it, but this gift was a person—a friend, a counselor, a personal coach, your greatest fan, mentor, Savior, and biggest intercessor all in one.

This is what I imagined happened: Jesus said, *I know that I'm leaving you, but the person I'm sending you will not leave. He will come to stay. When you find yourself confused, not knowing what to do, don't worry because He will know what to do. When you find yourself alone and afraid, find courage because He will protect you. You will never be alone as long as you make room for Him. Host Him inside your heart. He doesn't only want to be close to you like I was; He wants to live in you so that wherever you go, He will also go.*

Create an atmosphere, an Eden in your heart, where He can take walks with you in the cool of the day. Build a sanctuary, a safe place for Him. He is excited to do life with you. I know this might be difficult to understand but try your best. I know He is going to look different from what you are used to seeing in Me, but when you see

Him, in reality, you will be seeing Me. It really is Me, just in a different form.

Create an atmosphere, an Eden in your heart, where He can take walks with you in the cool of the day.

The Bible tells us that on that day in the upper room, there was a sound like that of a roaring lion that entered the room. It was like a strong windstorm that occurred only in that room. The wind was touching, moving like fire through all the disciples. They all started speaking in a heavenly language. They were each having a unique conversation with their Creator. It was as if God was depositing secrets in them that carried the power to change the world.

After reading these books on the Holy Spirit, I said, *Lord, I want this. I want my own upper-room experience. I create an atmosphere that will attract a fresh wind of Your Spirit. Do it in me, Lord. Let it be evident without a doubt that there's a fresh move of Your Spirit in me. This is what I need to become rich. This is what I need to be wealthy.*

I also read *The Deborah Mantle,* which empowered me to receive the anointing I need to fulfill the different roles God has equipped me for. It gave me the prophetic strategy to accomplish the assignments I'm about to step into. I don't know exactly what they are, but I know they are big.

Sarah Jakes Roberts released a word in her book that my spirit was ready to receive. I am the type of person that has the character of perseverance. **Perseverance is my message.** I am always in running mode: *You've got to keep pushing. You cannot quit. There is no time to rest right now. You've got to keep fighting.*

But what if I get tired? Don't you think there will come a time when I will get tired of always pushing? Will there not be a time to just relax? To just take a walk instead of a run? I felt the Holy Spirit tell me through Sarah's book, *Your season of perseverance is about to end. You can't always keep pushing through the labor pains and give birth to nothing. Your time of giving birth is around the corner.*

I felt the Lord was telling me, *this fast was your final push. You're about to live the season you have been waiting for. Peace is what's next. Get ready to enjoy the harvest.*"

For the scripture says, *"You must not muzzle an ox to keep it from eating as it treads out the grain."* And in another place, *"Those who work deserve their pay!"* (1 Timothy 5:18 NLT)

As I write this paragraph, I want you to know that I'm so excited! I believe it and I received the word. Sarah Jakes said if there is a word that is released towards you, you better make sure and catch it. Don't let it fall.

I will do whatever it takes to protect that word and see it come to life. You better believe I will protect it. You better believe I will use it and activate it. I will not only do it for myself but for my girls and for my family. We have paid a very high price to step into this season.

I am living the best version of myself as of now. You couldn't have met me at a better time.

I don't know what the future holds for me, perhaps more children, a bigger platform, or even a bestseller. But what I do know is
that God's plans are good regardless of my wants and desires.

In September of 2023, I went to the biggest women's conference
in the nation, maybe even in the world. I attended Woman Evolve
which was hosted in Arlington, Texas at the Globe Life Field. The
place was sold out. 40,000 women attended that conference. It was
amazing. Can you imagine a whole stadium filled with a heart of
worship? 40,000 women from all over the nation attended this
place for one reason, the name of Jesus. It was beautiful to hear
the name of Jesus resonate and echo through that stadium.

I captured the vision. My mind expanded. I was inspired. I
was able to see myself in Sarah Jakes. She's a model and loves
fashion. She's anointed and bold. She struggles with doubt but
still manages to show up every time. Fear bombards her but her
courage leads her. She isn't your average preacher. She doesn't fit
your normal pastor's wife role. She's not in the background. She
initiates. She stands out. She leads. She sets the pace. I never knew
another me existed. I'm not trying to sound prideful, but I do
believe that I'm evolving into this type of woman.

I pray that you the reader, could one day be edified in this
capacity as I have edified this woman that impacted me. Why not?
I left there thinking, *Lord, if You can do it in her, you can do it in
me.*

**She struggles with doubt but still manages to
show up every time.**

My Opportunity to Sow

The conference started on a Thursday. Every night, they picked up a special offering. On the first night, Bishop T.D. Jakes picked up a specific donation of $1,000. I was totally ready to sow into this ministry. I related to the number 1,000.

I had just recently declared to a small group of women, *"My goal is to impact 1,000 women and help them become the best version of themselves in the shortest amount of time possible."*

I said, *"Lord, if I sow this seed, I label it with this prayer."*

The following day, Sarah Jakes picked up the donation. It was specific to the number 5. *"You can give $555, $5,555.55, or anything with a 5 on it."*

I also related to this donation. I said, *"Lord, if I sow this seed, I name it a seed of honor. I honor the anointing that Sarah Jakes operates in. I sow this seed believing that the anointing that I honor is the anointing that will follow me. Could I be that Mexican American who can impact her race just like Sarah Jakes has impacted the African American community? Maybe yes, maybe not. Regardless, I have the faith to believe that God can do it. Let His will be done."*

I don't want to hinder my potential because I lack faith. If you haven't seen greatness, perhaps you're missing radical faith. What is radical faith? It's no longer faith the size of a mustard seed—it's the type of faith that makes you the initiator. Like Peter, he looked for the impossible. Did you know that it wasn't even Jesus' idea for

Peter to walk on water? It was Peter who tugged on Jesus. *"Can I come to You?"* Jesus approved of his faith, and the miraculous occurred.

The last day I believe the offering had the number 10 in it. By the end of the conference, I chose to sow $555. The power behind your seed isn't really the quantity, it's the faith you pour into it to activate it.

I finally have the confidence to believe God could do this in me and even greater things.

When you think about the millionaire fast you may be led to think that you will receive millions. The opposite is the truth. Imagine you can get to the point where you can embrace a lifestyle of generosity, where your donations are no longer limited to what you can give but to what he can give through you. Generosity is actually one of those keys that can unlock the wealth that is destined for you.

Imagine you can get to the point where you can embrace a lifestyle of generosity, where your donations are no longer limited to what you can give but to what he can give through you.

Going back to my 40-day fast. It's been very exhausting. Physically it's been traumatic. I haven't been able to sleep. My body is so weak. I've lost a lot of weight. It seems like I dropped the weight a lot faster this time than last year. It's been extremely hard. I didn't think it would be this difficult. I've been wanting to quit multiple times already. It seems like every time I preach or work for the kingdom my nights get worse. I started feeling very nauseous. Hunger is no longer the problem. It's the feeling of wanting to throw up.

Will I be able to do it another day? This has been my thought every night. Spiritually I'm reaching my goals but physically I just don't think I can make it. My daughter told me from the beginning, *"Mom make sure you listen to your body. You don't want to get sick and die."*

I have little fat left to lose. Now my body is feeding off my muscles. I kind of started getting anxiety at night. "You can do this," I keep telling myself.

I'm on day 21 now. This means after this day I will step into a new zone, something I've never done. Remember the most I've done is 21 days.

It isn't getting easier. My body feels like it's drying up. The hardest thing has been the coaching sessions I'm doing. I must act and play a role as if everything is okay. To be honest with you I'm dying on the inside. This is hard. It's been very difficult.

Having to take a shower, get dressed and put makeup on as if I'm having the time of my life, is no joke. I do feel like I'm playing the part though. I don't think my clients realize I'm physically falling apart.

I'm on day 23. One of my clients sent me a message and told me we could postpone the sessions until I finish my fast. I declined. We were on a momentum. We couldn't just stop. We were reaching our goals and seeing this work. We had an empowering session.

I'm on day 24 now, I have a couple of sessions to do today. This day has been hard. I would say my toughest. I'm so thirsty. Even though I drink a lot of water, nothing quenches my thirst. This has been a huge obstacle because I have a really bad taste in my mouth. I'm not sure if you have ever experienced an extreme thirst that doesn't go away. This is me right now. I kind of felt like the Samaritan Woman that Jesus met at Jacob's well. Let me give you some context.

Severe Thirst

Jesus and his disciples had left Judea and were on their way to Galilee. But in order to get to Galilee they had to go through a Samaritan village. It was a long journey. So, they stopped at a rest area, Jacob's well, to get some water and some food.

The disciples went into the village to buy some of the Lord's food, Chick-fil-A of course—just kidding. Jesus stayed behind at the well to wait for them. That's when a woman showed up with her empty jars.

As she approached the well Jesus asked her, can you give me some water to drink. Irritated by his question she responded, "Why are you a Jew asking me a Samaritan for some water? You guys wouldn't be caught dead talking to us."

I visualize Jesus' response like that of a Mexican parent, "*hay hija, si tu supieras? Daughter of mine, if you only knew?*" If you only knew why I'm here. If you knew the gift God has for you, you would be asking me for some living water.

The woman was so confused. She obviously didn't know who Jesus was. She was so boxed in her physical needs; she couldn't understand what Jesus was saying. She was focused on everything Jesus didn't have.

First of all, Jesus was empty handed. He didn't have a rope or a bucket. How would he be able to give her this so-called living water?

Jesus made it clear to her.

Open the eyes of your heart so you can understand. Anyone who drinks out of this well is going to continue to grow thirsty. But the water that I have come here to offer you is not like the water of this well. This well you must work on getting the water out. The water that I am offering you is different. It's going to come to you. Just like I came to you today. It's like an artesian spring within you that bursts out.

Open the eyes of your heart so you can understand.

The Artesian Well

Now, let's look at an artesian well or spring. Artesian water is much more expensive than regular tap water. It is filtered naturally through underground rock and soil, making it pure, essential, and unique in taste. This water comes from underground aquifers, which are containers created naturally by different rocks, sand,

and minerals. These natural containers serve as storage units for the water. You cannot see these underground pools, but once you tap into them, they become a reliable source of water for homes, farmland, and various industries. Artesian water does not need to be pumped out; it bursts forth on its own through the pressures and positive energy created underneath.

Do you know where I'm going with this? Fasting is a guide that leads you to dig 100 feet within yourself until you hit that unique water supply—pure, filtered, and sweet. This valuable water isn't found outside of you; it's hidden beneath the layers of experiences you have had. Yes, you might have to take the first step to dig this well, or it may even form naturally through different life experiences. But what Jesus is saying is that once you have this well, you won't even have to work at drawing the water out. It's going to flow naturally. Creative ideas will spring out of you. Businesses, ministries, new inventions, books, music—they will all burst out of you.

Do you understand what I'm trying to tell you? The *Millionaire Fast* concept I want you to adopt is one that allows you to tap into these underground pools of wealth—carrying knowledge and opportunities. This water may not look like Benjamins. To be honest, you don't even want to focus on money. The way the economy is going, those dollars will soon be valueless. What we want is a source of wealth that will never lose its value. It's one that will never die or expire, leading you far beyond life on this earth and into eternity.

Going back to the fast, I was physically thirsty.

My night was tough. I felt so much pressure in my heart. I was filled with anxiety. I was having a hard time breathing. I felt a little scared. I needed to have communion with Jesus. I took a cracker, and I blessed it, I declared Jesus you are the bread of life and as I take this bread I speak life. I was spiritually satisfied.

The following day, day 25, I made the decision to close my fast. I meditated on the word throughout the whole day and believed my sacrifice was fulfilled.

For those of you that know me, you know I am not a quitter. Quitting is not an option. You may think I failed but to be honest I felt accomplished. I'm glad I understood the true meaning of failure. Failure to me was simply not even trying. This was clearly not my case.

As I began my recovery, I kept thinking *"I wonder what I'm going to give birth to this time?"* The crazy part is that even my family and friends are excited to see what God will release over my life in this new season. Whatever it is, I know it's going to be good. Up to now God has not fallen short.

I wonder what I'm going to give birth to this time.

6

Risk The Comfort

"Fasting gives birth to prophets and strengthens the powerful. Fasting makes lawgivers wise. Fasting is a good safeguard for the soul, a steadfast companion for the body, a weapon for the valiant, and a gymnasium for athletes." — St. Basil the Great

This book is about **moments**—moments that unlocked hidden riches within me. It is not fictional; it's my story, filled with real-life experiences. This book is not a step-by-step manual on how to get rich. It is meant to inspire you to believe that you have a wealth of power within you, ready to be let loose. Fasting is one of the vehicles that will lead you to find those hidden treasures. This treasure does not look like silver or gold; it's much more unique and distinct. It is priceless; *"pure and undefiled, beyond the reach of change and decay"* (1 Peter 1:4 NLT).

It had been two months since I had finished my fast. That fast was an unforgettable experience. It had been the hardest one yet—to the point that I told myself, "I will never do this again." But now, as I reflected on what I had discovered, I found myself keeping that option open. I was ready to truly live out my earthly name. I knew God had been intentional when He gave it to me.

Are you living up to your name?

Have you ever stopped to think about what your name means? Your name identifies you. It describes what type of character you are in one word. That's why names are very important. A name attracts what it defines. Coral is a unique name. I've only met one person with that name—and that was recent.

When I was a little girl, I remember I really disliked my name. No one could ever pronounce it right. I disliked the first day of school, and the days we had substitutes were the worst. They always pronounced it wrong, and the students would laugh. I was already a shy person, embarrassed by everything, and that just added to my insecurity. I remember I was about eight years old, and we were in North Carolina for my cousin's wedding. One of the members of the church asked me, "*What is your name?*" I responded quickly, "*Jazmin.*"

My mother overheard me and said, "*That is not true. Tell them your real name.*"

I was so embarrassed—I was caught lying. I lied because I didn't like my name. Jazmin was my cousin's middle name, and I wanted it to be mine.

Living Up to the Name

My brother Rolando brought the meaning of my name to my awareness, so I began to research it. Corals are sometimes mistaken for rocks because of their hard surfaces. They are also seen as plants because they are attached to the sea floor. But, unlike rocks, corals are alive. I didn't know this, but they are animals.

First things first: corals are beautiful. Their wide range of colors catches your eye—they stand out. That's definitely me with my different hair colors. They also move, which was something I didn't know. This was interesting. In other words, they aren't stuck in one specific area. When they are little, they have the ability to move and grow.

Corals are foundational. They provide homes for 25% of all marine life. These homes serve as breeding grounds; hence, multiplication occurs. They are essential to planet Earth. It is estimated that half a billion people rely on coral reefs for food and work. Coral reefs are protectors. They protect coastal communities from strong storms. In other words, they take the first hit. They also work as a filtration system, cleaning the water they inhabit.

Corals live a long time. They are sometimes known as an underwater pharmacy with many medicinal benefits. Coral reefs thrive in areas where the current is the strongest. This is strange but impressive. Coral reefs need to be protected—they are threatened by climate change, pollution, and overfishing.

I remember telling my dad once:

"*Whenever you are present at church, I feel like I can do anything. It's like when my husband backs me up—I feel able to fulfill my assignment.*" I realized that my name was imprinted on my identity. Like corals, I thrive when I feel protected.

Now, I can tell you I'm ready to embrace my name. I'm ready to be a fountain of blessings to those around me. I'm ready to be that artesian well that can provide for entire communities. I believe I was created with a great purpose—to impact an entire generation. I finally believe every word God has spoken over my life.

Those strong currents were not meant to make my life impossible. They were actually meant to strengthen me and create something unique out of me. There is not another Coral on this planet. I am ready to press on those built-in settings and use them to their fullest potential. I didn't know what these buttons were for, but now I know—they were meant to unlock the supernatural essence of Jesus over my life.

The Courage to Walk on Water

Have you ever thought about the fact that Jesus walked on water? How did He do that? This was a phenomenon—something impossible, unnatural, and unheard of. But He did it, and guess what? He wasn't the only one.

The Gospels tell us that Peter challenged Jesus. Can you imagine having the courage to challenge the Messiah? He told Him, "*Lord, if it is really You, call me to come to You.*" I can just imagine Jesus' thoughts.

Like my friend Wicho says, "*No sabes,*" which means, "*This guy is about to find out.*"

Jesus' response was, "*Come.*"

Omg. Will he be able to? This is nerve-wracking but exciting. Peter stepped out of the boat. Focused on Jesus, he started walking toward Him. Peter walked on water! Yes, he sank afterward, but who cares? Regardless, he walked on water. He was the only courageous one who stepped out in faith. Yes, he was afraid, but he still did it.

This is the type of courage I need you to step into. Yes, you may be afraid, but that should not stop you. If worst comes to worst, you sink, and Jesus saves you.

That's exactly what happens in life. You may go bankrupt, you may have gotten a divorce, you may have lost an opportunity or missed the train. But when you get to the point where you feel like you're drowning—gasping for air—you can call on Jesus, and you better believe He will save you. He is the lifeguard on duty at all times of your day. You can trust Him.

Test of Faith

One of the first conversations I had with Jesus on the 40-day fast was, "*will I be able to fulfill this fast?*" his response was, "*Not by yourself.*" You can say well then where was Jesus. You didn't even finish it.

Do you remember the time God asked Abraham for his son to be given as a sacrifice? God didn't want him to kill Isaac. What He wanted was for Abraham to know what he was willing to do for Him. Abraham was all in, and he realized this when he was willing to obey and trust God. At the end, God provided the sacrifice, and Isaac lived.

Do you understand what I'm telling you? In other words, it does not matter what you may face in life. If Jesus is with you and you trust Him, you ought to know that even that which was meant to kill you will be used to promote you and give you life. I didn't have to do the 40 days; I learned I was all in by day 25.

Faith and Sacrifice

I'm tapping into a greater level of faith right now. Faith is a supernatural weapon in your favor. It activates the unnatural and produces the miraculous. Faith is simply complete trust or confidence in God. It's based on evidence but without complete proof.

"And it is impossible to please God without faith. Anyone who wants to come to him must believe that God exists and that he rewards those who sincerely seek him." (Hebrews 11:6 NLT)

I understood that God wants to reward me. I hadn't been able to have children for a long time, but I discovered something that shifted my life.

So, what will I give birth to this time? What will the reward look like? I thought I would have to tell you in my next book, but there is no need.

Guess what? God did it again. **I'm having another baby!** I still can't believe it. Could God do it again? Yes, He can.

I wasn't looking for it. I didn't fast to be able to conceive again, but God knows my greatest desires. Not only that, but I'm also giving birth to twins. These don't look alike, but they were inside of me at the same time. One of them is coming in the form of this book, and the other is a little human.

We recently celebrated my husband's achievement—a second master's degree. I told him, "*I'm so proud of you, and I'm ready to have more children with you.*" Everyone laughed, of course. At that time, I didn't know I was already pregnant. It materialized.

I have my third child. I don't know the gender, but whatever he/she is, I'm excited to embrace it.

To be honest with you, we had been trying to conceive since Zerah was born, and again, nothing was happening. We tried for almost one year. It wasn't until I finished my fast that it happened.

I don't know why it's more complicated for me to conceive. I don't know why I have to go through this crazy sacrifice. But I'm so glad I agreed. I discovered life—wells of life. I discovered the miraculous. My children are a product of faith and sacrifice. I gave my heart to God, and in return, He gave me His.

A Heart for God

I believe this is what happened with David. The Bible says that David was a man after God's own heart. In other words, David was constantly chasing God. He was constantly looking for God. David wrote and dedicated hundreds of songs to God. He went to sleep thinking about God. He woke up excited to be with God.

David wrote, *"You satisfy me more than the richest feast. I will praise you with songs of joy. I lie awake thinking of you, meditating on you through the night. Because you are my helper, I sing for joy in the shadow of your wings. I cling to you; your strong right hand holds me securely."* (Psalms 63:5-8 NLT)

I like to think of David like Zerah is with Pablo. She literally clings to him and doesn't want to let him go. She loves her dad so much she can't stand being away from him. Pablo laughs and says she is borderline toxic.

This was David. He loved God so much he couldn't stand the thought of being away from Him. He writes in another Psalm, *"Do not cast me away from Your presence, And do not take Your Holy Spirit from me."* (Psalms 51:12 NKJV)

I gave my heart to God and in return he gave me his.

I need you to understand when I fast it's never with the purpose of getting something out of God. I know along the way I've tagged my fasts with prayers, but this is not the reason why I fast. When I fast, I'm intentional about giving myself to him. My goal has always been to have quality time. Through this action I tell him, Jesus I'm putting my love into action. I never want it to be mere words. I need to show you with my life. I don't have much but I give you what I have, my heart.

Let's Go Deeper

You know how I tell you I'm not normal? We have started the New Year already. Guess what we do as a church in the New Year? We fast. We do *The Daniel's Fast* together. Don't tell me Coral, you're doing it? Yes, I am. My pregnancy isn't my excuse, it's my reason. Just look at all he has done for me.

I'm rich! I discovered the cure to barrenness. I tapped into the wells of riches hidden within me. This book is meant to shake the norm. This book is meant to help you step out of the box. Dare to believe that there's more for you.

We recently hosted our first women's retreat. This is an intense retreat targeted to deliver, heal and empower women into their destiny. God expanded my mind that weekend. He stirred up my heart to ask him for a specific prayer request. I asked him for seven children.

Why seven? "*Dude your obsessed. You're crazy,*" you may think. You are probably right. I am.

Dare to believe that there's more for you.

I don't know exactly why seven. But seven (7) is the number of completion in the Bible. I never thought I could have seven children. The whole time, I was just thinking, *One more, Lord.* But seven? That's hilarious, yet it feels so good just to have that hope.

Imagine —my dream is to fill this earth with God's riches. Those riches are found in the essence of Jesus deposited in each child I give birth to. Just thinking about who they will become fills me with joy.

I have an anointed preacher already—Galilea. Zerah is a warrior and intercessor; she knocks down Jericho's walls with her daily shouts. The baby on the way could become an entrepreneur creating opportunities for the kingdom. The others? A doctor, a heavenly worshipper, a writer, a composer, an engineer, or an inventor who will reveal heaven's secrets on earth.

I intend to create Eden—a garden-like environment of dominion and fruitfulness. This is the millionaire concept I've been trying to explain to you. It has nothing to do with money but with heaven's currency: **faith**.

Faith is the hope to believe that your imaginations can become reality. This book is a setup. God is setting you up for your greatest wins in life.

This book is a set up. God is setting you up for your greatest wins in life.

Faith Without Works is Worthless

There's an interesting story in the Bible about a demanding prophet and a poor widow. The story starts with the prophet Elijah proclaiming a drought throughout the land. He directly declares to the king of Israel, "*—There will be no dew or rain during the next few years until I give the word!*" (1 Kings 17:1 NLT)

Elijah prayed, and his prayers were answered. The question is, why is it that when we pray, nothing happens? My brother Manny explained in one of our empowerment sessions at church that Elijah lived a life of prayer. First, he prayed for no rain, and it didn't rain. Then he prayed some more. This time, he prayed for rain, and it rained.

The question is, how can I pray powerful prayers the way Elijah prayed? I believe consecration is a key to effective prayers. Being set apart for God means your focus is solely on Him. There are no distractions—nothing can be more interesting than the heart of God.

That's why riches are risky. The money, the fame, the influence, and the power can lead you to believe that it's you, and you forget about the Giver of it all. So then, why *The Millionaire Fast*? I don't get it.

I'm trying to tell you: *The Millionaire Fast* has nothing to do with money but discovering the heart of God and the purpose hidden within you—your original self!

In my first book, *Self-Doubt Out: God's Masterpiece*, I shared that one of my greatest battles is self-doubt. I battle thoughts of not being good enough. The truth is, I am not. But He is! That's what qualifies me. It's His goodness, not mine.

There was a question on the study guide of *Do The New You* that said, *Are there any areas where you feel weak, insufficient, or less than?* My response was quick: Yes, plenty. I feel I'm a good preacher, but not enough. We haven't been able to grow out of our current building. We haven't seen the breakthrough. It seems like we grow, but then people leave. So, the numbers just stay consistent. They don't increase.

I heard Jenny Weaver say this: she heard the Lord tell her, *"I've hesitated on giving you The Revival Center because I'm afraid of losing you. Right now, you are my girl, but will you still be mine when I give you more?"*

I understood what God was telling me. *Coral, right now you are mine, but when I give you the breakthrough, will you still belong to me?*

Sometimes God waits on the breakthrough because He knows there's a risk. He doesn't want to lose us. It all goes back to character. Our original must operate so that we can see what God has for us. The fall made us selfish, but the original takes us back to selflessness.

Sometimes God waits on the breakthrough because he knows there's a risk. He doesn't want to lose us.

The Prophet Elijah

Elijah communicated with so much boldness and courage. The word that was released obeyed his command. There was no rain for three years. As soon as Elijah declared this to the king, the Lord told him to go hide.

I know it doesn't make sense. First, he stands boldly, not caring that he is speaking to the king, and the next moment, God asks him to hide as if he were a coward.

Why Did God Ask Elijah to Hide?

I believe God was trying to protect him from the nation's influence. The people were going to get desperate and stressed out because of the drought. Whose fault would this be? Elijah's, of course. He is the one who made this proclamation, and the elements obeyed him. More than likely, they would have visited him, putting pressure on him to take back his words and proclaim the rain.

Too much pressure can definitely make us break. So, to prevent Elijah from giving in to this pressure, God told him to go hide by a brook. He clearly stated not to worry about food—the ravens would feed him.

What? Ravens? That's odd. Ravens eat everything, even the dead. They are unclean animals with dark hearts. How would this work? If I were Elijah, I would have lots of questions for God. But the story tells us Elijah obeyed.

Elijah did indeed have the essentials. He had food, water, and shelter. The ravens fed him twice a day. He slept in a cave nearby. There was plenty of water in the brook—until it dried up.

Oh no! It's like you're always on a rollercoaster ride with God. You're bold, then you're afraid. You're powerful, then powerless. There's plenty, and then there's lack. It's as if your spirit and flesh are taking turns. They are in and out.

When you're walking in the Spirit, the supernatural manifests. But then your flesh kicks in, and the natural takes over. Everything seemed fine until the brook dried up.

God's Next Instruction

God told Elijah to move again. He said, *"Go move in with a widow woman in the town of Zarephath. I already told her she needs to take care of you."*

What? This doesn't make any sense either. Widows are the ones who need to be taken care of, not the other way around. Remember, pure and genuine religion means caring for the widow and the orphan. Nonetheless, Elijah obeyed.

As he made it into town, he saw a lady gathering some sticks. She was preparing to make her last meal. The drought had been so bad that she was down to her last morsel of bread.

Elijah approached her and asked, *"Ma'am, can I have a glass of water?"*

The lady turned around quickly to get him some water. But as she stepped away, Elijah interrupted and asked her, *"I don't mean to intrude, but can I also have a piece of bread?"*

I can imagine she had been meditating on her devastating situation. She had no husband, no support system, and was living in the worst recession her nation had experienced. She looked in her pantry and saw she only had a handful of flour and a little bit of oil. She was the provider in her home, and there was no provision. Her heart and mind were filled with desperation. Her life was coming to an end.

So, when Elijah asked her for a piece of bread, she quickly responded, *"I swear by the Lord your God that I don't have a single piece of bread in the house. And I have only a handful of flour left in the jar and a little cooking oil in the bottom of the jug. I was just gathering a few sticks to cook this last meal, and then my son and I will die."*

The Prophet's Response

But Elijah said to her, *"Don't be afraid!"*

What do you mean? How could I not? Those would have been my thoughts. Is this guy not seeing the times we are living in? At the end of the day, it was his fault we were in this mess. He prayed for no rain, and there was no rain.

Elijah continued *"—Go ahead and do just what you've said, but make a little bread for me first. Then use what's left to prepare a meal for yourself and your son."* (1 Kings 17:13 NLT)

Omg! Are you serious? Is this guy crazy or what? Did he not hear what I just said? I don't have any food. I have one last bite of bread for myself and my son. And then he says bake the bread, but give me some first, and then you can eat the leftovers. What leftovers? There are not going to be any leftovers.

Sorry, I'm interrupting the story with my thoughts. I guess I just want you to understand her.

After Elijah told her to first give him the little piece of bread that she had and then eat the leftovers, he clearly declared it. I'd be ready for this response—the last time he declared something, nature obeyed him.

He said to her, *"For this is what the LORD, the God of Israel, says: There will always be flour and olive oil left in your containers until the time when the LORD sends rain and the crops grow again!"* (1 Kings 17:14 NLT)

She did exactly what the prophet told her to do. What happened next was out of this world. The story tells us that even though she poured out the flour and the oil, it never ran out. Not only did she provide for herself and her son, but also for the prophet. They had enough for days, weeks, and months.

Trusting God with the Little

Her situation was pretty scary. Her end had arrived until God interrupted it.

This is what can happen when you gain access to the currency of faith. You change your destiny. The impossible takes place. The supernatural occurs. Your chances change.

When I read this story, I felt God telling me, *"Coral, I don't care how little you have. Serve me with it. I know it doesn't make sense to give up the little that you have because that only means you will be left with nothing. Those are the results of natural business deals, but I am not your average entrepreneur. If you partner up with me, and you're willing to risk it all for me, worst case scenario is that I'm going to take care of you, your children, and your children's children. You won't have a need for money."*

"Come, all you who are thirsty, come to the waters; and you who have no money, come, buy and eat! Come, buy wine and milk without money and without cost." (Isaiah 55:1 NIV)

If I can be honest, I don't own much. I didn't own anything at all up until this month. My husband just finished paying for our car. What I do want to tell you is that when I fast, I always tell God, "I don't have much to give you, but I give you what I have, and that is my heart."

Risk the comfort. Willingly tell God, "I'm ready to delete all that I know to learn the truth. I'm ready to discover heaven's secrets and activate them in my very own household."

I'm ready to delete all that I know to learn the truth.

7

Completion
Perfection
Wholeness

"Fasting and prayer are key to bringing revival. It
is the most powerful spiritual discipline of all the
Christian disciplines." — Billy Graham

We have made it to the last chapter of this book. As I prayed this morning, I told the Holy Spirit, "*Let your breath spill like ink all over these pages and make it a masterpiece anyone can own.*"

A masterpiece is an outstanding work of art. It doesn't mean it's perfect, but it is done with excellence. The millionaire fast isn't a get-rich-quick scheme, nor a step-by-step list of how to get rich. It also isn't a specific fast itself, but the faith used when you do any type of fast.

I was remembering the first dry fast I did. This was something I had never done. Everyone's thoughts on it were negative because you don't eat or drink any water. Remember, our body is made up of over 70% water.

This fast was the first one I did while separating myself. My husband rented me a hotel room nearby. I really needed some time alone, just for God and me. When we read about fasting in the Bible, it's usually a time of repentance and used as a sacrifice to keep God's anger away.

It's normal for people to fast when something is wrong, when they face problems they cannot fix, and are in need of God's support. It's normal to fast when the only thing that can fix your situation is a miracle.

Fasting is a way to get God's attention for a specific purpose. The children of Israel fasted with Esther when Haman wanted to annihilate the whole race. Nineveh fasted when God himself was going to destroy the nation. Their fast was a form of true repentance.

Sometimes Christians fast for healing for a friend or relative. Others fast for a financial breakthrough or for the salvation of a specific organization or church. Some fast when they are living the darkest season of their life, like a loss, divorce, or some type of legal problem.

The Most Powerful Fasts

The most powerful fasts that I have done were when everything was right—when my life was in order, and I needed nothing. The best results I had were when I had no other intention but to have my Heavenly Father so close. There was nothing I wanted to get out of Him but simply to be in His presence.

Going back to that dry fast—I've done this fast three times. The first time I did it, I felt it was the hardest one, up until I did this last 25-day water fast. I was so thirsty. I never knew how much I needed water until I couldn't drink it. I wasn't hungry; food wasn't really a problem. It was the fact that I couldn't take a sip of water. I fell asleep thirsty. I woke up thirsty. In my sleep, I was thirsty.

I had to endure. It was only for three days, and I couldn't give in. For those of you who don't drink much water, I guarantee water will become your best friend the moment you cannot have it. During this fast, I sang the song *"I Love You, Lord"* repeatedly. I'm telling you; I wasn't in need of an answer. All I needed was Him.

I wasn't in need of an answer. All I needed was Him.

The Upper Room Experience

I pray this book can create that *upper room* experience that will empower you to step out in courage and materialize those riches trapped inside of you. I am now holding on to my wealth. I didn't even think this would be possible. I'm holding on to my third child. Coral went from having just one child to now embracing her third.

Just yesterday, I enjoyed my second-born holding onto my hand as she leaned toward my chest. I had to stop to take in the moment. She's, my miracle. If I had not fasted those 21 days, I don't think I would have ever experienced this moment.

My Why

As I am working on this book, Zerah is trying to get my attention. I literally had to stop to explain to her that I'm trying to share our story with the world. I picked her up and sat her right in front of me. She reminded me of my *why*. The *why* I'm writing this book, the *why* I am a mother, the *why* I am a pastor, the *why* I get up every day believing God for a supernatural moment. He's done it before. He can do it again.

I need the world to know that I am the richest woman in the world. My children are the best thing that could have ever happened to me.

The Miracle of Zerah

Zerah is now 2 years old. You would never guess what her first word was. You would think that because I carried her in my womb for 10 months—literally 41 weeks—and breastfed her, her first word would be *mom*. Well, it wasn't. She said *papa, papi, dada, dad, pa,* and every other way you can say dad. She never said *mom*.

It was not until she turned two that she said, *Bob*. Yes, *Bob*. Who's Bob? Well, that's me. Close enough. I accept it. *Bob* was the cutest word she had ever spoken. It has the greatest meaning. Most wouldn't understand unless you knew my story. *Bob* to me means purpose. It means wealth and legacy. My miracle is calling out to her mom.

Right now, she may not understand, but what I want her to know is that *mom* will be available to her and her sisters as long as God gives her the license to be on this earth.

Zerah woke up with a smile for the first year of her life. I remember posting daily stories of her smiles. It got to the point that everyone following me on social media got the phrase stuck in their heads, and they would repeat, *"¿Estas contenta?"* which means, *"Are you happy?"* She was happy, but I was happier. I was witnessing my miracle on a daily basis.

A Hope for the Future

My little one, Coral-Samaria is four months old now. I have the hope to dream and envision her future. Who will she become? What type of impact will she make?

I heard a podcast with Carl Lentz and Mike Todd. I'm not sure if you know who they are, and if you do, please give yourself the opportunity to learn from them. Mike said, *"If you read the Bible,*

true riches are people. The test of money is to see if you can handle
money so you can actually be trusted with people."

So did Jesus tell his disciples:

"If you are faithful in little things, you will be faithful in large
ones. But if you are dishonest in little things, you won't be honest with
greater responsibilities. And if you are untrustworthy about worldly
wealth, who will trust you with the true riches of heaven?" (Luke
16:10-11 NLT)

Those girls are what makes me wealthy, and the impact they will
cause is what feeds my faith.

What Are You Missing Out On?

As I said earlier, if I wouldn't have adopted fasting as part of my
lifestyle, I would be missing out on those hugs and those kisses I
receive from Zerah. I would be missing out on that beautiful smile
she gives me that says, *"Everything is okay, Mama."* I would be
missing out on the opportunity of sharing this story with you.

Let me give you a quick testimony. The other day I stepped into
the gym. As we were stretching, this beautiful tall woman came up
to me and said, *"I finally did it."* I was a little confused about what
she was talking about. It was 5 a.m., and I was still trying to wake
up. She said, *"I'm the one that messaged you about the fast."*

I automatically remembered someone messaging me on Insta-
gram about two years prior. She had seen a post I shared about the
21-day fast and my miracle baby.

I said, *"Yes, I remember."*

She told me how she had attempted the 21-day fast a few times, but she couldn't complete it. She failed time and time again until she finally did it. She tagged her fast with a specific prayer request. Her daughter was born with a lot of health issues. Three years had passed, and she was not able to walk nor talk. Her condition was severe. She prayed and fasted, asking God for her healing.

As she was telling me, there was a big smile on her face. *"My daughter now walks. Her condition isn't perfect, but I do see her progressing."* She was inspired to believe that God could do it if she activated her faith by doing this fast. I awakened a hope in her that otherwise would have stayed dormant.

The Cost of Sacrifice

One of my friends invited me to join her in a podcast about fasting. She was interviewing me, but toward the last minute, I ended up interviewing her. I was so impacted by one of her moments after a fast, I wanted everyone to know.

In 2023, she went to a tent revival in Tennessee. It was a deliverance conference. During the last day of these sessions, she felt the Holy Spirit ask her to give up her phone. She didn't understand why God would be asking her for her phone if, a few months prior, she had sown a special seed asking God to help her grow her social media platform.

What do you mean a seed? She made a pact with God by giving a special offering. This topic of **Pacting** is a discussion within itself, which I will cover extensively in an upcoming book.

She was fighting the thought of surrendering her phone, but before the service was over, she walked up to the altar and placed it on that platform. She thought this was crazy. How would she communicate, how would she work, how would she do anything? Nowadays, we do everything on our phones. She traveled back home without a phone and was phoneless for a month. I remember calling and texting her during that month and getting no response.

To add to this sacrifice, she felt God ask her to fast for a whole month. She did a liquid fast where she only drank juices and water. So, for the whole month, she was away from social media, without a phone, and without solid food.

What happened next is crazy. The day she got back online, she found out there were thousands of dollars that her previous videos had generated. Her social media platform exploded in the following months. She made so much money, she had enough to buy her own home. Yes, you heard me.

This act of faith and obedience unlocked a treasure that had been there all along. So why would God ask her to give up her phone when that was exactly what she needed to reach her goals? Was it a test?

It's as if God was asking her, *do you trust me enough to give up what you've been asking me for?* I believe God wanted her to know who the source of her prosperity was when she got it.

It reminds me of Abraham and Isaac. God's plan was never to take his son. God wanted Abraham to recognize the extent of his own willingness to do whatever it took for God's will to be accomplished. That act of faith made Abraham the wealthiest man ever to exist. He became the father of God's dream. His act of faith unlocked a nation that was in him.

A Church Revived

Let me share another testimony. It was a country church home that was struggling to stay open. The community needed it, but there were just no financial resources to keep it alive. It was once full of life. Fresh paint filled the halls, children ran around in the playground, while the young adults studied their Bible.

One of the members of this church knew that change was necessary, but what direction would they take? This had been her home for the past 15 years, and it broke her heart to even think that the possibility existed that she would show up on a Sunday and the doors would be closed.

She felt it in her heart to go on a 40-day journey with God. She did a 40-day water fast, praying for revival and a clear direction.

So, what were her results after this fast? It hasn't even been three months, and the church has taken a big turn. New families have been added to the congregation. The donations have increased. This past month, they surpassed their giving budget, which they hadn't met for the past four years. People now want to give and have activated themselves to serve in the areas that had been empty for years. The church has revived and is filled with hope now.

My Husband's Breakthrough

One of my husband's goals for this year was to retreat by himself and fast. Half of the year had passed, and he had not even put a date on it. A week before he went back to work after being off for the baby's birth, I asked him, *"If you know that fasting works and that God has so many rewards—especially His presence on that journey—why wouldn't you take it? Think of your daughters. They are so young, and they need their father to live a long life for them."*

He automatically took the call and made the decision to fast for five days. He called his brother to ask if he could stay at his dad's house, where he had spent his last years of life. His brother gave him the green light.

Monday came, and he left. I felt pain for him. I wanted him to do this, but I knew it would be painful. It wasn't going to be easy. This was his first time doing this type of fast.

I know I'm writing this book because I want you to practice this principle, but at the same time, I would rather fast for you. I would rather go through the pain than you have to go through it. But I know that's not how it works. We each have to pay the price so that we can find its value.

When my husband came back home, he looked so humble. He did lose some weight—his legs were skinnier. As he took time to reflect on his experience, I asked him, *"What did you receive? What did God show you?"*

He responded, *"I felt that God set me apart to close a chapter in my life—mourning my father, which I hadn't fully done since his death two years ago. When he passed, I felt I had to be strong for my family, the church, and myself. I carried that weight for so long, and God set me apart in my father's house to understand what he experienced in his final stage of life. Before this, I couldn't imagine myself growing older, but now I feel I will age gracefully and see my children grow up joyfully."*

My husband had mentioned to me before that he couldn't see himself being old. In other words, when he meditated about his future, he didn't see himself reaching an old age, as if he would die prematurely. This fast allowed him to unlock his future. He tapped into a season he thought would never happen. I truly believe Pablo will grow old and see his girls become who God sent them to this earth to be.

Casting the Net

Writing this book hasn't been easy. It's taken me about a year and a half to complete. My season hasn't been the easiest. I've had moments where my purpose has been challenged. At the beginning of the year, I was in a partnership that I thought would last a lifetime. That partnership broke before the summer. It didn't even last a year. I remember losing my breath, sobbing in my living room, asking God, "If you knew this wasn't going to work, why did you allow me to go through with it?"

Jesus said, "*Anyone who comes to me but refuses to let go of father, mother, spouse, children, brothers, sisters—yes, even one's own self! —can't be my disciple.*" (Luke 14:26 MSG)

We must be willing to surrender all, and by *all* it means everyone who means the world to you. It's not that Jesus wants to take them from you; it's that He wants to show you that, yes, even though they do play a part, they don't *make* you. Coral isn't Coral because of her husband, her pastor, her friend, or her father. Coral is Coral because God created her and formed her. Coral will exist because of God and not anyone else. Your identity will never come from a person, no matter how much influence they have on you. Your identity comes from God, the One who ordained you to be.

Those moments when departure happens are painful because you never imagined it would be necessary. But even these moments are crucial for your growth and maturity. I haven't really talked about emotional healing in this book, and I would love to take this time now. A healthy heart is the foundation for living a rich life. Fasting has allowed me to truly forgive those whom I perceive have harmed and betrayed me. I made the choice to destroy every list of grievances that I had made. I don't need to live my life reminding myself of all the harm people have caused me. That takes my joy, robs my peace, and doesn't let me do my assignment with excellence.

If you are a person who carries a lot of resentment and is constantly focusing on the offenses you carry, I want you to consider this: Would you like God to carry a list of grievances you've caused Him? Would you like Him to remind you every time you've betrayed Him and offended Him? I suppose you wouldn't. So then, why carry a list yourself? Wouldn't you be happier focusing on all the good that has occurred in your life? I'm not saying ignore your feelings. All I am saying is to direct your attention to those moments that have built you.

When Jesus left this earth, the disciples were heartbroken. Their teacher, the one they had spent the last three years with, was gone. No more meals together, no more walks, no more sleepovers, no more adventures. No more moments. They didn't know what to do anymore. Peter couldn't take it and decided to go fishing. This is what he used to do before he met Jesus—he was a fisherman. A few of the disciples joined him. They fished all night and caught nothing.

Does this sound familiar? This was Peter's story before he met Jesus. He had no results, and now he was back to that life again. When the sun rose, someone shouted at them, *"Friends, do you have any fish?"* They answered, *no.* Then He said the words that opened their eyes: *"Throw your net to the other side."* There were so many fish, they couldn't haul the net. Instantly, Peter knew it was Jesus. This was exactly what happened when he first encountered Him—a miracle catch.

Peter quickly threw himself into the water and swam to shore. Here is where Jesus asks Peter three times, *"Simon, son of John, do you love me?" "Peter, do you love me?"*

He answered, *"Yes, Lord, you know that I love you."* Jesus responded, *"Then take care of my sheep. Feed them."*

This weekend, I received a revelation for my season. I heard Jesus tell me, *"Cast the net to the other side,"* and you know what? I trust Him. There's a miracle catch waiting for me. And like I've told you before, He's never fallen short.

I'm casting my net through this book, believing that *you* are part of my miracle catch. I know God has called me for this, just like He called Peter.

My response is, ***"Yes, Lord, I love you."***

What opportunities are waiting for you, hidden in plain sight, that require your spiritual eyes to be opened? At first sight, Peter had no idea it was Jesus calling out to them. It was not until he witnessed the catch that he realized it was Jesus. He remembered those were the same words He told him when they first met.

At this point, the Holy Spirit may be shining His light on that treasure within you. You may be receiving revelation about something God had already spoken to you about, but you hadn't yet comprehended it. It's really nothing new because it's been within you this whole time—you just weren't aware.

I pray that you are able to discover for yourself the power of fasting. May the Holy Spirit prepare the right time this year so that you can have your own *upper room* experience. I would love to hear your story. I would love to hear your testimony on how you acquired your wealth.

Key Takeaways

Benefits of Fasting

Fasting is a powerful tool that impacts every area of life—spiritually, physically, and mentally. Below is a summary of the key benefits of fasting covered in this book:

1. Spiritual Benefits

- Increases Clarity & Connection with God – Removes distractions and enhances spiritual sensitivity.

- Strengthens Faith & Discipline – Helps build resilience and trust in God's provision.

- Brings Breakthrough & Acceleration – Many experience answered prayers, divine insight, and supernatural encounters.

- Purifies the Heart & Mind – Fasting exposes and removes hidden struggles, allowing personal transformation.

- Aligns You with God's Purpose – It helps reposition you for growth, purpose, and calling.

2. Physical Benefits

- Detoxifies the Body – Eliminates toxins, supports liver function, and enhances overall health.

- Boosts Energy & Longevity – Stimulates ketone production, reduces inflammation, and can slow aging.

- Aids in Weight Loss & Metabolism – Promotes fat burning while preserving muscle longer.

- Rejuvenates Cells – Activates autophagy, a process that repairs damaged cells and promotes healing.

- Enhances Mental Clarity – Removes brain fog, improves focus, and sharpens memory.

3. Mental & Emotional Benefits

- Builds Self-Control & Discipline – Strengthens the ability to resist cravings and distractions.

- Reduces Stress & Anxiety – Creates a sense of peace by aligning thoughts with purpose.

- Breaks Addictions & Unhealthy Habits – Resets cravings and helps remove unhealthy dependencies.

- Boosts Creativity & Innovation – Many report heightened problem-solving abilities and new ideas during fasting.

Bonus Material

F asting is a spiritual discipline that trains your mind and body to focus on God's purpose for your life. Through fasting, you extract the impurities and distractions that hinder your growth, allowing the essence of the Spirit to shine through.

Fasting is more than a temporary deprivation of food—it is an invitation to reset, refocus, and transform both the mind and spirit. In today's world, where distractions are abundant and goals often feel out of reach, fasting provides an essential opportunity for clarity and reflection. It acts as a bridge between where you are and where you want to be, a tool that sharpens your spiritual and mental faculties.

The first step in fasting is understanding its purpose. While many view fasting as a religious or physical practice, its roots go deeper—it touches the core of self-mastery. Fasting strips away distractions, clearing the path for a more focused approach to life. It's a conscious decision to say "no" to temporary comforts so that you can say "yes" to long-term success.

This practice is about refining your inner strength, much like athletes training for a marathon. The discipline you build through fasting is not unlike the endurance training needed to push beyond your limits. And, just as an athlete rises to meet a challenge, fasting helps you rise to the challenge of achieving your highest potential. The discomfort that often accompanies fasting is an integral part of the transformation process. It is in the discomfort that true growth happens.

Notes

R eferences
    Ajmera, Rachael. "8 Health Benefits of Fasting, Backed by Science." *Healthline*, medically reviewed by Amy Richter, RD, Nutrition, 23 Apr. 2025, https://www.healthline.com/nutrition /fasting-benefits. Accessed 19 June 2025.

    Brandhorst, Sebastian, et al. "A Periodic Diet That Mimics Fasting Promotes Multi-System Regeneration, Enhanced Cognitive Performance, and Health span." *Cell Metabolism*, vol. 22, no. 1, 2015, pp. 86–99. *PubMed Central*, https://doi.org/10.1016/j.c met.2015.05.012. Accessed 19 June 2025.

    Longo, Valter D., et al. "Intermittent and Periodic Fasting, Longevity and Disease." *Nature Aging*, vol. 1, no. 1, Jan. 2021, pp. 47–59. *PubMed Central*, doi:10.1038/s43587-020-00013-3. Accessed 19 June 2025.

    The Holy Bible: King James Version. Thomas Nelson, 1987.

    Holy Bible, New Living Translation. Tyndale House Publishers, 2015.

    Xin, Lijing, et al. "Nutritional Ketosis Increases NAD^+/NADH Ratio in Healthy Human Brain: An In Vivo Study by 31P-MRS."

Frontiers in Nutrition, vol. 5, 2018, article 62, https://doi.org/10.3389/fnut.2018.00062. Accessed 19 June 2025.

"This book is so deeply personal and vulnerable that I at times felt intrusive on Lisa's inner world and her pain. I, like many others, felt the compulsion to "look away" from the deep grief expressed because it made me feel things too. This is the beauty and message of this book. Don't look away; instead, be with. Sit with the grieving and sit in your own grief. Let it hurt and don't hurry it along. Grief is a wound that can be transformative, and as Lisa unpacks her journey through piles and piles of hurts and calls attention also to the glimmers in their midst, the reader summons the courage to walk on in their own journey. They become fellow travelers, just as Lisa comes alongside others in her healing work with Grief Guide. I recommend this book for anyone needing a raw, honest guide who can help them gather their bravery to move in some of the darkest mires they may ever face."

Dr. Caitlyn McClure, DSW, LCSW
Vice President of Clinical Services
Northern Illinois Recovery Center

"I have known Lisa for many years as a pastor, colleague, and friend. Her story of grief is honest, tender, and deeply compelling. I'm grateful for her vulnerability in sharing not only how she continues to navigate loss but also the resources that have sustained her along the way. Equal parts memoir and guide, Lisa's story beautifully reflects the steadfast love of God, the power of community, and the sacred work of healing. Her words invite us to honor our own journeys of grief with courage, grace, and hope."

Rev. Tammy Swanson-Draheim
President, Evangelical Covenant Church

A Letter from Monsignor James Shea

Dear Lisa,

Thank you for sending me a copy of your book, *Never Apologize for Your Tears*. I read it with interest. I was especially moved by your recounting of Kierra's passing, as it was an event that deeply affected our community at the University of Mary. We did our best to rally around Michael during that deeply sad moment and in the days and months that followed.

Your poignant reflections on your time spent with our Benedictine Sisters at Annunciation Monastery were very beautiful. The Sisters are, as you say, a quiet and hospitable refuge for those who need to step in out from the wind for rest, prayer, and silence.

May this book—clearly the fruit of your own grief journey—give hope and light to many others in this needful, broken world. And may God bless you!

Monsignor James Shea
President, The University of Mary
Bismarck, North Dakota